Whoever Tells the Best Story Wins

*How to Use Your
Own Stories to
Communicate with
Power and Impact*

SECOND EDITION

Annette Simmons

⁴AMACOM

American Management Association
New York • Atlanta • Brussels • Chicago •
Mexico City • San Francisco • Shanghai •
Tokyo • Toronto • Washington, D.C.

Bulk discounts available. For details visit:
www.amacombooks.org/go/specialsales
Or contact special sales:
Phone: 800-250-5308
E-mail: specialsls@amanet.org
View all the AMACOM titles at: www.amacombooks.org
American Management Association: www.amanet.org

This publication is designed to provide accurate and authoritative information in regard to the subject matter covered. It is sold with the understanding that the publisher is not engaged in rendering legal, accounting, or other professional service. If legal advice or other expert assistance is required, the services of a competent professional person should be sought.

Library of Congress Cataloging-in-Publication Data

Simmons, Annette.
    Whoever tells the best story wins : how to use your own stories to communicate with power and impact / Annette Simmons.–Second edition.
        pages cm
    Includes bibliographical references and index.
    ISBN 978-0-8144-4913-4 (hardcover)–ISBN 0-8144-4913-1 (hardcover)–ISBN 978-0-8144-4914-1 (ebook)–ISBN 0-8144-4914-X (ebook) 1. Business communication. 2. Storytelling. I. Title.

    HF5718.S562 2015
    658.4'52-dc23

                                                                                    2014046423

About AMA
American Management Association (www.amanet.org) is a world leader in talent development, advancing the skills of individuals to drive business success. Our mission is to support the goals of individuals and organizations through a complete range of products and services, including classroom and virtual seminars, webcasts, webinars, podcasts, conferences, corporate and government solutions, business books, and research. AMA's approach to improving performance combines experiential learning—learning through doing—with opportunities for ongoing professional growth at every step of one's career journey.

Printing number
10 9 8 7 6 5 4 3 2

Contents

PART THREE   *Perfecting the Craft*

Acknowledgments

FOR THIS SECOND edition, I offer a big thank-you to Danuta Electra Raine, Stephen Brewer, and Martin Karaffa. It is wonderful to have such smart, generous friends!

Introduction

THIRTY YEARS AGO, stories were mainly for kids and oral history nuts. Now the word "storytelling" defines a comprehensive communication strategy that blends principles of emotional intelligence, education, entertainment, and neuroscience for applications as varied as law, marketing, organizational development, leadership, health care, and user-based design. Storytelling went viral.

This is hardly surprising. Technology dumps so much information on us; we now need a conscious process to translate that information back into the human brain's inborn format for understanding the world: into story. The science is in. The brain thinks in stories. Since my first book on storytelling, *The Story Factor*, came out in 2000, I've witnessed communications of every kind improve when people learned how to craft and share a story that feels personally significant to both sender and receiver. Stories replenish information with the food of human connection and reignite powerful motivations stimulated when we feel the sense of our shared humanity.

Once you know how to find and tell stories that feel personal to you *and* your listeners, you have the basic skills necessary to acknowledge, connect with, and emotionally move others. The best storytellers learn to use their own emotional responses as divining rods to locate and tap into the emotional responses of others.

When you practice telling your own personal stories, you learn what kind of details make a story come to life. Telling personal stories gives you valuable practice using various sequences and sensory details to construct new contexts. Most of all, telling personal stories gives you authentic feedback from real live humans instead of hypothetical guesses that may or may not match actual responses.

When the sense of human presence is distilled out of our attempts to communicate by ill-conceived conveniences or even well-intentioned formats, it deadens the impact of that communication. There are enough formats claiming to have identified the "seven elements of a viral video" or "five attention-getting headlines" to prove there is never one clear path to achieving the real goal of human connection.

Most storytelling advice has you constructing a story from the *outside in*. All stories share certain elements. For instance, every story has a plot, characters, setting, conflict, and resolution. Well, sure it does, but that doesn't stimulate an emotional connection—it just gives me a plot, characters, setting, conflict, and resolution. On the other hand, telling personal stories teaches you storytelling from the *inside out* by putting emotion and personal connections first. Unless you bring a beating heart to your message, it is dead. But when you tell your own heartfelt stories about what is meaningful in your life and work, you get the hang of finding stories that frame life and work in emotionally meaningfully ways for your audience.

Telling personal stories helps you put experience into perspective. For instance, say you tell a story about an unhappy customer who heard that someone bought the same car he or she did for half the price. This customer was satisfied with the purchase again after hearing the half-price story was a rumor, but not quite as satisfied as he or she was before hearing the falsehood. Such is the power of story to interpret experience— never hearing about the half-price deal, or hearing it was a rumor from the get-go, would trigger a whole different set of responses (pleasure that a customer is satisfied) than hearing the false story that led this poor person to believe he or she had been a sucker (sympathy with someone who's been duped). Likewise, a "man-stabs-son" story could be interpreted as a murder or as a life-saving emergency tracheotomy. Telling personal stories teaches you that every audience is full of personal stories you can tap into to create comfort or play off of to create surprise and suspense. The old rule to "know your audience" becomes a much more fertile exercise as you adopt a storytelling approach to communication.

When you have cultivated the habit of personal storytelling, you are more likely to come up with story ideas to make your presentations personal and emotionally engaging. After a year of blogging personal stories about his hospice volunteer work, a real estate friend was inspired to use storytelling to prove to a city council that he genuinely appreciated the historical significance of the piece of land he wanted to develop. He asked local school kids to draw pictures depicting the historic events and used their drawings in his PowerPoint presentation. In the past, he might have stuck a historical timeline lifted from the city's website into his slide deck. Instead, he enjoyed a couple of hours at a local school giving and getting a history lesson from third graders—the teacher thought it was a great idea—and they were happy to share their drawings. A few weeks later, he got his building permit.

To understand the power stories wield is both an incredible opportunity and an awesome responsibility. Please use it for good, not evil.

In the first edition of this book, I quoted Barry Schwartz, author of *The Paradox of Choice: Why More Is Less* (New York: Echo, 2004), to demonstrate that we need stories more than ever to help us make good choices and stay satisfied with them. He wrote, "There's a point where all of this choice starts to be not only unproductive, but counterproductive—a source of pain, regret, worry about missed opportunities, and unrealistically high expectations." The ocean of choice is only getting bigger, and we need the life preserver of meaningful stories more than ever.

Since then, Schwartz and coauthor Kenneth Sharpe wrote a book titled *Practical Wisdom* (New York: Riverhead, 2011) in which they explore the inadequacy of our attempts to use algorithms to capture and replicate wisdom. Wisdom is situational, and algorithms have trouble when the answer is "it depends." Zappos (the online merchant) discovered that stellar customer service is a result of stories and culture rather than some algorithmic script for call-center employees. Zappos customer-service representatives have no scripts. Instead, they are encouraged to be creative and adapt a personalized approach to each customer and situation based on core values. Managing with stories can feel like flying without a net, but our safety nets of algorithms, policies, scripts, and rules only support the illusion that consistency translates to quality. When it comes to emotions, consistency translates to apathy. Stories are more agile and adaptive for interpreting the best response to the kind of diverse and unique situations we encounter in our highly ambiguous and emotional world.

Aristotle noted that craftsmen don't measure curves and indentations with a straightedge. Rather, they use a tape measure that bends and molds to forms. No matter how refined an algorithm or formula is, it can never match the flexible personal wisdom embedded in stories that can bend and mold, innovate, and improvise.

Once you develop your innate talent of understanding the world in terms of the stories we tell ourselves, you gain access to deep currents of wisdom that help you communicate better and more authentically. Despite decades of pretending our work isn't to be taken personally, storytelling proves that if it isn't personal, it doesn't matter.

PART 1

Thinking in Story

CHAPTER 1

Story Thinking

OUR FIRST STORIES come from our families, and they are intensely personal. My mother's father died six months after I was born; yet through Mother's stories, I feel as if knew my grandfather. He sold Kellogg's cereals in the 1940s and 1950s. He was outgoing and loved practical jokes. I have a photo of him sitting like a general atop a pony so short his weight is not even on the animal. One of the stories Mother told me includes a joke he loved to tell. The punch line is at the heart of my book's premise.

A man walks into a pet store and says, "I want a talking parrot."

The clerk says, "Yes sir, I have two birds that talk. This large green parrot here is quite a talker." He taps on the cage, and the bird says, "The Lord is my Shepherd, I shall not want." "It knows the entire Bible by heart. This red one here is young but he's learning." He prompts,

"Polly want a cracker." The bird repeats, "Polly want a cracker."

The man says, "I'll take the younger one if you can teach me how to make it talk."

"Sure I can teach you," says the pet store owner. He sits down with the man and spends hours teaching him how to train the parrot. Then he puts the bird in the cage, takes the man's money, and sends him home to start the training regimen.

After a week, the man comes back into the store very irritated.

"That bird you sold me doesn't talk."

"It doesn't? Did you follow my instructions?" asks the clerk.

"Yep, to the letter," replies the man.

"Well, maybe that bird is lonely. Tell you what. I'll sell you this little mirror here and you put it in the cage. That bird will see its reflection and start talking right away."

The man does as he was told. Three days later, he was back. "I'm thinking of asking for my money back. That bird won't talk."

The shop owner ponders a bit and says, "I'll bet that bird is bored. He needs some toys. Here, take this bell. No charge. Put it in the bird's cage. It'll start talking once it has something to do."

In a week, the man comes back angrier than ever. He storms in carrying a shoebox. "That bird you sold me died." He opens the shoebox, and there is his poor little dead parrot. "I demand my money back." The shop owner is horrified! "I'm so sorry, I don't know what happened. But tell me . . . did the bird ever even try to talk?"

"Well," says the man, "it did say one word, right before it died."

"What did it say?" the clerk inquires. The man replies, "It said: 'Fo-o-o-o-od.'"

Poor parrot, he was starving to death.

That parrot needed food the way we need meaningful stories. People are starving for meaningful stories, while we are surrounded by impersonal messages dressed in bells and whistles that are story-ish but no more effective than giving a mirror and bell to a starving parrot. People want to feel a human presence in your messages, to taste a trace of humanity that proves there is a "you" (individually or collectively) as sender. Learning how to tell personal stories teaches you how to deliver the sense of humanity in the messages you send.

Whether your goal is to tell brand stories, generate customer stories on social media, craft visual stories, tell stories that educate, interpret user stories for design, or build stories that explain complex concepts, the exercise of finding and telling your own stories trains your brain to think in story.

Story thinking maps the emotional, cognitive, and spiritual world of feelings. For humans, feelings come first. We destroy facts we don't like and elevate lies that feel good. We've tried to control this tendency by teaching ourselves to make more rational, unemotional, and objective decisions. It's worked pretty well, but if all you have ever been taught is to make unemotional, objective decisions, your capacity to stir emotions, see stories, and understand the logic of emotions may be underdeveloped or nonexistent. This book gives you new skills in story thinking that will complement your skills in fact thinking. Facts matter, but feelings interpret what your facts mean to your audience.

How to S.E.E. Stories

Any significant emotional event (s.e.e.) can be a story. Similar to shifting between yin and yang, right brain and left brain, or art and science, the following image demonstrates how you can't see two frames of reference at the exact same time . . . You can go back and forth as fast as you like, but in the instant you see the people the vase disappears and vice versa. It is the same when we s.e.e. stories. We may have to allow the data to become ambiguous for a second in order to discover a story that provides new context and enough meaning to change how people interpret the data.

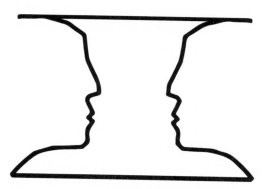

Once you learn to flip back and forth between objective thinking (the vase) and story thinking (the people), you can present the right answers in a way that not only is factually correct but feels right too. If the right answers were enough, everyone who needs to lose weight would only ever have to read one diet book. Behavior change requires more than knowing what to do; we have to *feel* like doing it.

Story thinking may feel a little scary to the average business mind because it calls for us to temporarily lay objective thinking to the side and look at the stories, metaphors, analogies, and intuitions that explain emotional responses. Much like the vase/people picture, we can look at one and then the other, granting them equal time and then blending the wisdom of both. Compared to facts, stories look ambiguous and inconsistent. We must seek to understand emotions by learning to speak the ambiguous, variable, and unsteady language of emotions—the language of story.

The emotional payoff of a powerful story warrants the act of letting go of critical thinking long enough to find a story. Do we need expensive quantitative data analysis to find ideas more easily discovered by feeling our way through stories? Recently, a quantitative analysis of data from employee name badges embedded with microphones, location sensors, and accelerometers revealed that productivity goes up and turnover goes down when you replace the fancy coffee machine reserved for senior executives with a shared space encouraging unstructured, 15-minute coffee breaks for everyone. We need only to seek stories about inclusion and exclusion to find ways to improve engagement and save our research money for experiments.

Story thinking happens naturally as you gather and tell stories that simulate the kind of life experiences that people consider to be meaningful. If something feels meaningful, it is meaningful because of the story we tell ourselves about it. Stories track patterns of interpretation that people, institutions, and cultures weave around events. Stories hover over the facts and draw lines of connection or disconnection—good, bad, relevant, or irrelevant—to create personally interpreted meaning.

What's Important and Why

Every culture is based on stories and metaphors that aggregate around that culture's preferential answers to universal but ambiguous human dilemmas like how to manage time, authority, safety, money, ethics, and whatever else is important. If it is important to the culture, you will find a story that tells you what is important and why. In Russia, I was told how real estate contracts were simply voided when a better offer came in because "Russians play *with* the rules rather than *by* the rules." As an American, I have my own biases, but this story clearly told me what to expect and how to act.

Lots of wonderful things become possible with story thinking. When you know what you *should* do, but don't *feel* like doing it, calling up the right story can tip the balance in your favor. When I teach storytelling to executives, some on the edge of burnout, they report a surge of energy and appreciation after sharing stories of why they chose their occupation.

Writing about an unexpected text message from a mentor who typed, "I totally adore you," magically changes how I feel. Later, when I shared this boost with my friend at lunch, it changed how he felt too. He smiled as I shifted from feeling stressed to basking in adoration.

Notice what happens to your physiological state, attention, emotions, and behavior when you remember your first love. How old were you? What hairstyle and clothing were you wearing? Picture the attention you gave every interaction, potential interaction, and fantasized interaction. Stay there until you feel a ghost of the feelings you felt then. Have you smiled yet? Do you feel a slight urge to action? Perhaps you want to discover where your long lost love is now.

Now steel yourself for a less pleasant trip. Go back to high school and pull up a memory of an embarrassing rejection. Any public humiliation will do—just choose one. If you are like most people, high school was full of them. Give that embarrassing memory all your attention. Remember the names, see the places, and reenact the scenes. Now notice the ghosts of the feelings you felt then as they reignite. You may feel a tug toward actions that prevent this kind of experience. This experiment demonstrates how attention—in this case, attending to a memory—alters your current reality by changing how you feel.

The key to story thinking is to learn which stories stimulate your own feelings first. Then find the stories that also stimulate the feelings of others. The skills you develop by starting from the inside will help you learn the way stories create the feelings that motivate us to action.

Story Thinking Is Not the Opposite of Objective Thinking

Learning to think in story does not erode your ability to think in objective terms. You can still conduct a cost/benefit ratio analysis with the best of them. If you naturally use objective tools such as root cause analysis or statistics to identify "right" and "wrong," it may be uncomfortable to flip into subjective mode. It is important to remember that we don't abandon objective logic and measurable outcomes when we think in stories. We complement objective facts with the kind of story thinking that tracks emotional and perceptual patterns in others and ourselves. Story thinking explores the fact that people can make the right decision for the wrong reasons and opens our eyes to see how wrong can be good (watch much reality TV?) and right can be bad (patenting a cure during a pandemic) without forcing an oversimplified resolution or averaging extremes into zero.

Some gifted individuals seamlessly process objective and subjective factors as easily as a child prodigy plays the piano. The rest of us lean to one side or the other. Western education tends to produce more objective thinkers. The style of right-brain thinking, artistic interpretation, and the hidden world of yin are so similar to story thinking they can sometimes feel interchangeable. In other words, if you are already a master of left-brain, science-oriented, yang energy, then story thinking is your fast track to find more innovative, human-centered ideas and make better emotional connections.

Relax Your Internal Critic

Your internal critic might seek to discredit story thinking as too subjective, irrational, or corny. Stories are a hot topic right now, but the process of finding and telling stories is old fashioned—prehistoric, in fact. Objective thinking tempts us to update this process with technology, automation, or measures. Beware: you may just destroy that which you seek to understand.

I'm not a fan of techniques that try to turn the subjective nature of stories into modules, recipes, or tactics. I hear people say stories always have a beginning, middle, and end. Hell, what *doesn't* have a beginning, middle, and end? Likewise, you can have a plot, characters, themes, and crisis and still not have a good story. Whatever interaction simulates a visceral, experiential sense of meaning—to the satisfaction of the listener *and* the teller—is a story.

Stories don't just map the way humans thought before we discovered science and technology. Stories represent the way the human brain *still* thinks. The first step is to suspend objective thinking and find the source code of human emotion: experiences. Stories are encoded by the social and emotional brain, the limbic system, the amygdala, and the other core parts of the brain that trust the five senses more than symbols such as numbers or an alphabet. Here, numbers and language do not represent physical reality as well as memory and images do. These parts of the brain treat experience as the best teacher. Stories are only one step removed because stories are simulated experiences.

Stories do not obey traditional rules of logic, and they can change your interpretation of what is meaningful and important in the wink of an eye. It's disconcerting at first, but once you get used to it, you discover this is the magic of story thinking.

> An old farmer patiently spent part of each afternoon talking with a nosy neighbor, who visited him about the same time every day. One afternoon during his daily visit, the neighbor suddenly exclaimed, "Did you buy a new horse? Yesterday you only had one horse, now I see two."
>
> The farmer told the neighbor how this horse, unmarked and apparently without an owner, wandered

into his barn. He explained that he had asked everyone he knew, and since no one owned the horse, he decided he would care for it until they found its owner.

The neighbor said, "You are such a lucky man. Yesterday you had only one horse and today you have two." The farmer said, "Perhaps, we shall see."

The next day, the farmer's son tried to ride the new horse. He fell and broke his leg. That afternoon the neighbor said, "You are an unlucky man. Your son now can't help you in the fields." The farmer said, "Perhaps, we shall see."

The third day, the army came through the village looking for young men to conscript to fight. The farmer's son was not taken because he had a broken leg. The neighbor again said, "You are a lucky man," and again the farmer said, "Perhaps, we shall see."

Think about the time wasted arguing about what is or isn't true, when it all depends on the stories we tell ourselves. The farmer was unlucky and lucky, depending on the story. Both are true, depending on where you are in the story. Story thinking adapts decisions and implementation strategies to suit changing points of view rather than forcing all ambiguities to resolve into the false clarity of the lowest common denominator. We know everything will change tomorrow anyway, so we may as well lean on the things that don't change—meaning and universal truths. Stories that are emotionally stimulating relay truths that were true before you and I were born and will remain true long after we die.

The Western world has spent a lot of time and energy learning how to exclude emotions from decision making, but decisions that ignore emotions are easily ignored in return. Story thinking doesn't bring emotions *back* to decision making, but it gives us *access* to the emotions that have been there since the beginning of human history.

Thinking in stories can feel dangerous or unstable, but as a psychiatrist friend of mine put it, a blind man who could suddenly see would not poke his eyes out just because some of the things he saw were terrible. Stories simply reveal the patterns of emotional reasoning where they lay so you can see the best possible route to where you want to go.

This book is designed to help you lay the groundwork for using stories as credible tools. Understand that allowing the emotions back into decision making can be very destabilizing for people whose entire lives are designed to be objective and rational. Storytelling in a work situation can awaken long-denied emotions about personal decisions in a way that may frighten people who convinced themselves that emotions don't matter. Be gentle. Stories are very powerful tools. When you activate new stories, you transport people to new points of view and change meaning and behavior, and in that way, you change the future.

CHAPTER 2

Story Is Experience Reconstituted

EXPERIENCE IS THE best teacher—always has been, always will be. Experience changes minds, alters decisions, and creates cohesive action.

If we could magically transport the people we wish to influence into a life-changing experience, we could change the world. Imagine a software engineer suddenly transplanted into a client's daily life where he or she personally experiences the frustration of bugs in the system he or she designed. Better yet, let's transfer a politician into the body of a low-income, single mother's life for just one day. It's a sweet fantasy to imagine this person—someone who doesn't even pick up his or her own dry cleaning—shopping in a supermarket with three unruly children and trying to buy fresh fruits and vegetables on minimum wage. Would he or she ever forget that experience?

Direct experience is the Scrooge method of education: transport a shortsighted boss, coworker, customer, or teenager to a place and time that leaves an indelible experience in the deepest parts of his or her brain. Far below the conscious level of intellectual knowing, personal experience delivers deep understanding that allows true empathy and challenges the false clarity of entrenched positions or slick politics. Put an investor to work in a sweatshop in an underdeveloped country and then ask if it is possible to better monitor suppliers' working conditions.

Yet this best tool to influence others—personal experience—isn't feasible in most cases. Even if a person desperately needs to see outside his or her narrow point of view, kidnapping is strongly discouraged. The best you can do is bring these transformational experiences to life with a story that is so vivid, so impactful, it feels as if the listeners were actually there. For them, a story becomes a type of personal experience, even if it is experienced vicariously. This is why I define *story* as a reimagined experience narrated with enough detail and feeling to cause your listeners' imaginations to experience it as real. There are other literary and grammatical definitions of story that are helpful, but this definition keeps you focused on stories that influence and change perceptions.

You may not realize how often or when you share your experiences—but every story you tell contributes to the story bank people use when interpreting new information. Every war story, anecdote, critique, or acknowledgment creates the cultural climate of your team. Nothing is more important to your success than the stories others believe about your work, personal, and community life. These stories even create the way your see yourself because they define how the world reacts to you.

Maybe your strategy has been to stick to the facts and data to keep emotions out of it. Nevertheless, experiences with big data prove that more data and more facts simply illustrate the law of diminishing returns by creating the emotional state we call "overwhelmed." Our brains create stories to make sense of complexity, and we are bombarded daily with data and personal experiences of escalating complexity. Our stories help us weight data as important (or not) as well as judge the data as good or bad according to our point of view. Complexity and ambiguity are now the norm, so without proactive stories, we leave it to reactive stories to create interpretations that may or may not serve the organization. The point is that it's to your benefit to be mindful of the stories you tell.

Stories We Tell Every Day

In a way, it's not necessary to *learn* storytelling because we tell stories every day. This book is actually designed to help you *pay better attention to the stories you tell*, so you can adjust the perceptions your stories build and sustain. Most of the time, we don't realize we are telling stories. It is even less obvious how powerfully these stories impact our lives.

Unfortunately, we usually tell stories about how stressed we are, how stupid some people are, or how no one on earth has ever had an airplane/airport experience worse than ours. Empathy is a rare resource in high-tech relationships. So many of us don't realize how often we use meetings and face-to-face conversations to vent frustrations or share war stories.

Now, we need to vent frustration somehow, and telling stories works, but not with people we want to influence.

You are *already* telling stories about who you are; why you are here; and what you envision, value, teach, and think about another's secret thoughts. The problem is that you haven't realized how much your stories matter. To help us pay attention, let's look at the six kinds of stories we tell that lead to influence, imagination, and innovation.

Who-I-Am Stories

What qualities earn you the right to influence a particular person? Tell of a time, place, or event that provides evidence that you have these qualities. Reveal who you are as a person. Do you have kids? What were you like as a kid? What did your parents teach you? What did you learn in your first job? Get personal. People need to know who you are before they can trust you.

Why-I-Am-Here Stories

When someone assumes you are there to sell an idea that will cost him or her money, time, or resources, it immediately discredits your "facts" as biased. However, you chose your job for reasons besides money. Tell this person what you get out of it besides money. Or if it is just about the money, own it.

Teaching Stories

Certain lessons are best learned from experience, and some lessons are learned over and over again—patience, for instance. You can tell someone to be patient, but it's rarely

helpful. It is better to tell a story that creates a shared experience of patience along with the rewards of patience. A three-
minute story about patience may be short and punchy, but it
will change behavior much better than advice. It is as close to
modeling patience as you can get in three minutes.

Vision Stories

A worthy, exciting future story reframes present difficulties as
"worth it." Big projects and new challenges are difficult and
frustrating for implementers who weren't in on the decision.
Without a vision, these meaningless frustrations suck the
life energy out of a group. With an engaging vision, however, huge obstacles shrink to small irritants on the path to a
worthwhile goal. But be careful, because Vision stories that
promise more than they deliver do more damage than good.

Value-in-Action Stories

Values are subjective. To one person, integrity means doing
what his or her boss tells him or her to do. To another, integrity means saying "no" even if it costs his or her job. If you
want to encourage or teach a value, you have to provide a
"demonstration" by telling a story that illustrates in action
what that value means, behaviorally. Hypothetical situations
sound hypocritical and preachy. Be specific.

I-Know-What-You-Are-Thinking Stories

People like to stay safe. Many times they have already made
up their minds with specific objections to the ideas you bring.

They don't come out and say, "I've already decided this is hog-wash," but they might be thinking it. It is a trust-building sur-prise for you to share their secret suspicions in a story that first validates and then dispels these objections without sounding defensive.

Choose the Stories You Tell

As mentioned before, if we were to judge people by the stories they tell on a daily basis, we would conclude most of them are stressed-out, misunderstood victims (Who-I-Am) here to survive red tape and stupid decisions (Why-I-Am-Here). They pine for retirement or the firing of a certain individual (Vision), and they believe that the "haves" couldn't care less about the "have-nots" (Value-in-Action). They unconsciously tell stories that ensure coworkers learn that no amount of effort is going to change things (Teaching) because they've already tried and failed (I-Know-What-You-Are-Thinking).

I'd like to encourage you to mindfully tell stories that will improve results you get at work, in your family, and in your community. When you turn your attention to the six kinds of stories I've just outlined, you will be more intentional in creating the kind of perceptions that achieve goals rather than reinforce problems.

Suppose you want to create trust with new employees or, more likely, with current ones disgruntled by the last reorgani-zation. The best way to build trust is through experience. No one will argue with that. People want to see us keep agreements, act with integrity, and hold confidences secure. But it takes a long time to build feelings of trust. It takes more time to wean off of the habit of second-guessing, arguing, or displaying passive resistance when trust has been broken.

And you need cooperation now. In most cases, people never get to see the when and how of you doing the right things, even if you did have plenty of time to let trust build. In real life, people rarely experience how you struggle to keep agreements, because they aren't there when this happens, nor do they see the ways you try to protect your people when you are overruled. Most people can never know what it cost you to go to bat for them—at least not firsthand. Unless you tell them the story of what happened, they only experience the incomplete and imperfect sample of who you seem to be in daily exchanges. They only see little glimpses of you—usually out of context—and these rarely showcase your better qualities because work is hard.

Think about a typical day. You wake up with great (OK, good) expectations of having a productive day. Then the kids spill their cereal and the dog jumps on your freshly cleaned trousers. Some idiot cuts you off in traffic. This day is up and down, like most days. You get to work, and the up and down continues. The phone rings with news that you got the big client you wanted. You decide to celebrate with the team at a staff meeting that afternoon; maybe you buy some doughnuts. Three hours later, after slaving over exhaustive and question-ably relevant reports due yesterday, you notice that a couple of staff members are putting golf balls in the hall instead of working. Suddenly, writing an e-mail to discourage play-ing golf in the hallway becomes your first order of business. Enthusiasm about winning the new client wanes, so by the afternoon, you forget the doughnuts and treat the staff meet-ing as just another staff meeting.

When, during this typical up-and-down day, does your team experience you? When you are happy, productive, and at your best? Or when you are disappointed and frustrated? Most of us have to admit we are not that noticeable when we are happy and productive. We sort of fade into the woodwork. The times we seek attention are the times when we think a correction needs to be made. Indeed, Western culture is almost addicted to correction. Monitor and correct. Monitor and correct. The problem with this is that people's experiences of you become skewed to the negative.

It's completely natural. Our brains are hardwired to pay more attention to problems rather than building relationships, teaching, communicating vision, daydreaming of innovations, or explaining misunderstandings. No one seems trustworthy anymore. If you don't like the facts on one TV station, you can switch channels.

In today's world, sticking to your facts and data will leave emotional reasoning untended. If you aren't telling stories with intention, you may be unintentionally minimizing people's feelings, passion, sense of purpose, and perceptions in a way that could generate negative perceptions and failure.

Your stories need to be more than intentional. They need to be personal. In truth, every story is already a personal reflection. Even a historical anecdote is personalized to your choices of what to include or exclude, your posture, and tone of voice. Many business stories fail if the teller is under the illusion that business isn't supposed to be personal. If you care about people, success, failure, growth, or any other aspect of the business, it's personal, so show it. Vivid, brightly painted stories can take staff into the room where big decisions were made. You can bring copies of flipchart lists that demonstrate conflicting and difficult issues. Tell of the long pauses, reflections, and tough conversations that occurred during deliberation. Describe how the team ordered pizza and kept working until 11 p.m. When people reject leadership decisions, it has a lot to do with not understanding how the process worked and not seeing bigger-picture issues. If you get in the habit of telling stories that take peers and staff (briefly!) back in time to see who, when, how, and where important decisions get made, you build trust that can serve in the inevitable situation when there is no time to explain. Someday, time limitations will force you to issue orders without explanation, and your team will infer that, like the others, your decision is based on the same diligent considerations they've come to know through your stories.

In order to jump-start your storytelling practice, chapters 5–10 will protect you from avoidable pitfalls and help you record what you learn and accumulate a bank of stories for future use. There is a chapter for each of the six kinds of stories, with ample opportunity to practice and cement the principles and philosophical approach that create good storytelling.

Each chapter gives plenty of examples and shows you where to look for your own stories. Take the time to jot down story ideas, test your stories, and record your reflections. By the end of Part 2, you will have developed a set of mental habits that ensure new stories are easy to spot, develop, and tell whenever you want to win hearts and minds to your point of view.

Once you get in the habit of seeing how stories shape perceptions, interpretations, lives, and businesses, you will see just how many opportunities you have to improve these perceptions, interpretations, lives, and businesses.

CHAPTER 3

Learning to Tell Stories

AN INVISIBLE WEB of stories determines who pays attention to you and what your messages mean to them. Imagine putting on a pair of glasses that reveals all these stories as little thought balloons over your own and your audience's heads, highlighting the shared and conflicting stories that will interpret what your message means. Once you can see these stories, it becomes obvious that the more stories you share the better your ability to communicate. You might choose to tailor your message to fit into an existing story shared by your audience or introduce a new story to redirect interpretation of existing circumstances, but once you see all the stories, you can never ignore them again.

If you have ever sent a message that was clear as day (to you) yet created the opposite of your intention, it is likely that you were blind to at least one story critical to your intended meaning. It isn't hard to see the stories that might distort your intended meaning, once you know how to look. Storytelling is as much a function of story finding as of storytelling. Sometimes you want to retell an existing story to apply a familiar context for new information. And sometimes you want to tell a new story so people can see what seems familiar in a new way. Stories can seem invisible until you get crosswise with one of them.

Story Awareness

Cultural differences help illustrate the effect of conflicting stories. At one level, that is all culture is: a collection of stories. In the United States, our stories teach us that if we blow our own horns and pull ourselves up by our bootstraps in order to be the early bird that gets the worm, we will succeed. But in a culture where group success is more important than individual success, introducing yourself to a group by sharing a long list of personal accomplishments tells the wrong story. In Japan, the story that points to success is that the protruding nail invites the hammer. In Australia, the story of the tall poppy syndrome clearly warns everyone that when they try to raise themselves above the rest, they are just asking to get their head chopped off.

Stories aid survival by recording a culture's best guesses to unanswerable questions so people can live their daily lives. At work, we can't collaborate smoothly without shared opinions on who, what, when, where, and how we define good and bad work and what it means to win or lose. Stories tie emotions to certain patterns so we don't have to wake up every morning and struggle with such existential questions as "Is the individual or group more important?" We just feel an emotion that moves us toward what feels "right" and away from what feels "wrong." These metaphors train people from each culture to feel the same way about individual and group efforts in a way that minimizes the number of potential conflicts in daily life.

Cultural awareness comes from learning which stories a culture uses to interpret big questions. Story awareness is recognizing that, even within your own culture, different points of view and significant personal experiences get soaked in positive or negative emotions, so when something similar happens again (or seems to happen again), emotional reactions preemptively propel us toward or away from what our stories say will happen next.

Story awareness helps you communicate better with people who don't think the way you do—which, by definition, includes anyone you want to influence. You may choose to tap into an existing story that invites listeners to interpret what seems unfamiliar with a familiar context or what seems familiar in an innovative (unfamiliar) way.

Most storytelling translates into telling a story that sets up your preferred context for interpreting a message. I told the parrot story at the beginning of this book to pull your attention to the familiar story that "we need human connection as much as food," along with a new story about "sharing stories as a form of human connection," so you might conclude that "we need shared stories as much as we need food." Someone might complain, "I don't need to hear about a man killing a bird," but that's the nature of stories—there are no 100 percent guarantees. Except perhaps that no story will ever match 100 percent of the people you seek to influence and that it is still better to tell a story rather than leave emotional interpretations to chance.

Storytelling is also a function of your ability to find current stories at play. For instance, if you want your staff to feel they are being treated fairly, it helps to identify the stories they tell to illustrate fair/unfair behavior. Their stories might imply that hard work should always be rewarded. Or maybe hard work doesn't matter because whoever brings in the most business should get the lion's share of the profit, regardless of effort. Then again, a good year may be interpreted as a windfall that should be shared equally, or you might work with a highly competitive bunch who tell war stories about getting there first, and those who snooze lose. Explaining a new compensation structure to a diverse group can be treacherous. I've heard that law firms usually have three compensation structures: the one they used to have, the one they have now, and the one they are planning to adopt because every compensation structure feels fair or unfair based on your story. Once you know which stories are popular, you can call attention to a fairness story that fits best by narrating a vibrant, visceral version of that story to direct perceptions and smooth the transition. Once you understand how stories create emotional reactions, how can you possibly leave these interpretations to chance?

You may choose to create an experience that gives people a new story to tell. Experience is still the best teacher. For most people, a picture of a suggestion box generates something between an eye roll and a "yeah, right" response. Stories of management ignoring or co-opting suggestions from the field may compete with your ability to tell the story "We want your suggestions and will reward you for innovation." When new stories compete with old stories, you may need to create a significant emotional experience juicy enough to be shared as a story. I heard of one senior manager who offered every employee two forgiveness coupons for any mistakes they might make trying new ideas *and* insisted that they use both by the end of the year. I can only hope that when employees tested his story by making mistakes they had good experiences and shared stories that confirmed this story was true.

Storytelling develops your radar for using stories to influence others. At work, any misunderstanding becomes an opportunity to both ask for and tell a story. Frustration with certain behaviors suddenly prompts you to try to understand the story that frames these behaviors as good or necessary in a way that either eliminates your frustration or enables you to try to influence their story with your own. You move upstream as you set conflict aside and instead negotiate a new cocreated story that can make everyone feel they are on the same team. The applications are endless, but let's start with the basics.

Storytelling Practice

Your goal is to tell a story that feels enough like a real experience that it stimulates an emotional response. Storytelling is part art and part experimentation. I wish I could give you forgiveness coupons because some of your stories will fail to achieve the results you desire. Or maybe you could give me some forgiveness coupons because like all innovations, storytelling feels risky and there will be hits and misses. Rule number one to deal with the misses is to adopt the discipline of telling stories that last at most three minutes. If it's a miss, it will be over soon and you can adapt and adjust.

I don't think it is possible to influence someone else's personal feelings if you aren't willing to share your own personal feelings. Your storytelling abilities will be directly related to your willingness to reveal your personal interpretation of events that shaped your own emotional reasoning. Storytelling is an "I'll go first" dance between teller and listener.

In order to go first, you need to find some good stories you can tell in low-risk situations. Understanding that you should be telling stories and getting to the point of actually telling stories can feel like a chasm to cross. This is the point at which we leave the hypothetical and get real. Your personal storytelling will be all about you, your stories, and your definition of *win*.

You may have noticed that this book offers no overt definitions of *winning*. Winning could mean that your efforts ensure a building project proceeds or that it is cancelled. Winning might mean your company doubles growth or that your company intentionally forfeits profit to achieve human rights goals. Your definition of *win* is up to you. Once you are clear on what you want to achieve and who you want to influence, it is time to begin.

Nothing will improve your storytelling more than practice. Personally experiencing your stories as they work their magic will be so gratifying that you won't have to remind yourself to include a story—it will become second nature. Initially, you may feel a natural hesitancy due to thoughts that include "I'm not a good storyteller," "This takes too long," "It is unprofessional to share personal stories," or "I have real work to do." These are escape doors to avoid discomfort, uncertainty, and risk. I know all about escape doors. As a writer, my mind offers escape doors such as "Have you checked your e-mails?" or "I wonder what an Internet search would turn up," or "Did you remember to turn the dishwasher on?" or the worst, "I wonder what is in the refrigerator?" At some point we have to decide to "just do it."

Where Do I Find Stories?

Researching on the Internet and identifying case studies or current events are good ways to find events that provide examples of your ideas. However, stories are more than mere examples. Winning stories feel personally significant to your listeners. The catch is, only by finding and telling stories that feel personally significant to *you* can you expect to elicit the level of personal engagement that wins hearts and minds. An emotional and personal connection is what engraves your meaning. When this meaningful point of view is imprinted, future experiences are more likely to flow along the channel of interpretation left by the story.

This is a subtle yet vital distinction often overlooked in professional settings. Some people think personal stories are inappropriate. Sure, there is such a thing as too personal—anything that makes people cringe or that generates shouts of "TMI!" (too much information) is too personal. However, most personal stories are perfectly appropriate whenever the discussion involves "persons."

One advantage of using personal stories is that they are easy to remember. After all, you were there when everything happened. When people ask questions, you can answer them. Curiosity is a vital goal of storytelling, and questions often follow a powerful story. If you are telling a story about Lou Gerstner at IBM, you may have trouble answering detailed questions (unless you *are* Lou Gerstner). In order to tell the story, you need to know the back story.

Authenticity-in-action means sharing personal stories or personal feelings about someone else's story. Sharing personal experiences earns you trust at the same time as you share information and exert influence. To simplify and accelerate your storytelling, I present four buckets of stories that tell who you are; why you are here; and what your vision, teaching points, values, and secret empathies are. The four buckets are the following:

1. *A time you shined.* This kind of story is about doing the right thing. If you are communicating a quality such as integrity, a value such as compassion, or a learning situation, these stories will tell about a time in your life when it would've been easier to do anything but the "right" thing. All the outside pressures told you to do one thing, but you did the "right" thing, and everything turned out for the best. You were tested and you took the high road.

2. *A time you blew it.* This is about a time when something bad happened and it was all your fault. It sounds backward, but telling a story that discloses a mistake can increase trust twice as fast as polishing the story to give it a professional finish. The very fact that you are sharing a personal failure, flaw, or embarrassing moment means that you trust your colleagues enough to go first. Trust often fails because neither side wants to go first. When you go first, you get the ball rolling, and people are more likely to trust you back. Don't worry that people will think you are a failure—successful people always have failure stories. This story works because people can tell how you felt about failing your own standards by the way you tell the story and the tone in your voice. It reveals your

character because it shows how hard you can strive to overcome and change.

3. *A mentor.* The third kind of story could be about an important person in your life or the personal impact of someone you may have never met. You are sharing an experience or a story that taught you something important in an effort to share the valuable lesson with others. Telling a story of admiration and gratitude toward another person who embodies the qualities or goals you value not only communicates these qualities and goals but also demonstrates to your listener the very important qualities of humility and gratitude. These two qualities are vital in good leadership. Humility and gratitude are the essence of personal dignity. Another advantage in telling a mentor story is that people often assume that you share these qualities, values, and goals. Particularly when you can't come right out and say "I'm humble," your stories can demonstrate that quality for you.

4. *A book, movie, or current event.* There are millions of stories from books, movies, newspaper articles, or other media sources that might just be perfect to make your point. There are even ways to make these stories personal. Find a scene from a movie, book, or current event that exemplifies what you wish to illustrate. Choosing a well-known book or movie takes advantage of all the hard work the author or director put into stimulating the senses and capturing attention. If you tell a story about the movie *Independence Day* (1996), you

don't have to conjure up special effects to blow up the White House because the director Roland Emmerich has already done it all for you. Make the story yours by adapting the format and style (including the details of how you came across this story) or by elaborating on what this story has meant to you and why you are sharing it.

These aren't the only places to find stories, but they may be the easiest. Let's leave it to the academics to pore over plot types and perfect arcs; you just need stories that deliver an emotional experience. As you read the examples for each of these four stories in this book, jot down as many ideas as possible that pop into your mind. Don't be inhibited by second-guessing yourself. Writing it down is no commitment that you will tell that story in public. Coming up with ideas is faster and more creative once you turn your internal editor off and your internal compass on. Inauthentic stories only happen when you try to hide who you really are or try to be someone you are not.

These four primary story sources are reliable for just about any situation. As you develop as a storyteller, you will become aware of your favorite sources, and by then, you'll have your own methodology. These four buckets will get you started.

Getting Feedback

If you can practice storytelling with a work group or as a part of a training class, you have ready listeners handy. If you are doing this alone, you will need to find one or more listeners who can resist the urge to "critique" your stories. This sounds wimpy at first—but stay with me.

Storytelling is more of an art than a science. The creative process thrives on a mysterious creative force that could be described as "feeling creative," "finding your inspiration," or "being in the flow." This creative force is a delicate and very subjective process. It's like a timid, wild animal you want to tame. Loud noises or sudden movements scare it off. Over time, you can domesticate it to some extent, but part of that process will be feeding it and learning what it likes. I have a writer friend who writes with five sharp number-two pencils and is completely put off if his wife sweeps away the eraser dust. Creativity comes to those who aren't afraid to tune in to their own eccentricities.

Critical feedback improves objective skills yet can kill subjective creativity if applied too soon. Professional artists sometimes seem eccentric to us because they have learned that their creative juices flow better with special treatment. Another metaphor that helps me is that a new story must be tended like a new fruit tree is tended by a gardener. The tree needs what it needs when it needs it. In the beginning, the tree needs water and light. It is too soon to prune. Pruning the tree can kill it before it has a chance to grow. Leave it in the dark for too long and it dies. Overwater it and it dies.

Think about your stories in the same way. They are little trees that first need water and light. Criticizing a story too soon just demoralizes the teller and invalidates the subject. Half the time, I think criticism is more about the critic than the subject of critique. If you are a perfectly secure, emotionally healthy person who is telling a story that does not carry any strong feelings, maybe you want a critique. But please don't let social pressures and ridiculous phrases such as "Don't take this personally" bully you into listening to criticism before your story is strong enough. Storytelling is personal—of course you are going to take it personally. That's why we are doing it. Storytelling brings personal engagement back into our organizations and social interactions.

The word *feedback* (as in "I need to give you some feedback") has become a socially acceptable term in some dysfunctional organizations for what looks remarkably like emotional abuse. As long as you make your living doing something other than storytelling, my advice is to ask to hear "what works." This is based on the appreciations model developed by Doug Lipman in his book *The Storytelling Coach*.[1] It takes more courage to ask for positive comments than it does to ask for feedback. This method doesn't work because it protects delicate egos. It works because it encourages the strong parts of your story to grow toward the light. Because it is too soon to prune, negative feedback kills a baby story. Negative feedback kills a story when it turns our attention to the wrong things instead of the right things.

Training a Listener

In order to test your stories, you need a listener or listeners. Practicing in a mirror or in the car alone is not good enough. A story is a cocreation in your mind and in the mind of at least one listener. It's not storytelling without a listener—it's acting, preaching, or something else. Your story should be different every time you tell it, in response to your listeners.

---

1.   Doug Lipman, *The Storytelling Coach* (Atlanta: August House, 1995).

You can't practice responding to your listener without a live listener.

For your first test telling, you'll want a "no-risk" listener. Recruit a friend, spouse, or coach who will agree to give you only positive feedback for your first telling of any story that you intend to use later in a higher-risk setting. The second telling can be at work or in a "real life" situation, but your first telling needs to be "no risk." Initially, we need to explore the story and develop our skills for telling this particular story.

No matter how skilled you are at storytelling, all stories can be distorted by premature feedback and suggestions. Sometimes negative feedback comes in the form of "Can I make a suggestion?" One time I got a "suggestion" and, as a result, I dropped a detail out of a story when next I told it. The story fell flat without it, so I put that detail back in. I've since come to the conclusion that the person who made the suggestion may have felt judged by his interpretation of what that detail meant. After reflecting, I realized that I wanted this detail to provoke self-examination. I had said, "Nasrudin had not prepared his words to touch the hearts and minds of the people; he thought he could wing it." My choice of wording makes "winging it" sound like an act of hubris. I'm OK with that. If I can save anyone from suffering through unprepared, stream-of-consciousness ramblings, it is worth it. Opening the floor to criticism often gives you more information about your listeners' pet peeves than the quality of your story. Appreciations are much more reliable in finding the parts of your story that work and letting the other parts die on the vine.

The secret of good storytelling is having the confidence to protect your creative process in the early stages from criticism—internal as well as external.

Use this format to ask for what works:

"What your story tells me about you is. . . ."

"What I like about your story is. . . ."

"What your story helps me remember is. . . ."

"The impact I can see your story having in a specific situation (describe) is. . . ."

It may feel manipulative asking only for positive feedback, but after a while you will see it actually takes more courage to protect your creative process—courage you can use in other situations to protect good boundaries.

CHAPTER 4

It's All Storytelling

AFTER 20 YEARS of teaching storytelling to executives, I've learned most of us were trained to use thinking habits that help us be more rational, more logical, and more scientific in our approach to work. Unfortunately, three of these thinking habits can also make you a lousy storyteller. The secret of becoming a good storyteller is to develop the ability to toggle back and forth between fact thinking and story thinking.

Specifically, you were taught the following things:

1. The value of a tool is a function of consistently reliable results (ideally greater than 90 percent).

2. Facts are more accurate and thus more valuable than anecdotes.

3. Solutions have a direct and logical relationship with the root cause of a problem.

4. Results correlate in proportion with effort and investment.

These habits protect you from low standards, taking things too personally, getting swept up by emotions, and from wasting time using a process that has to be redesigned every time you use it.

However, since our goal is to engage humans with an unpredictable set of emotional states in a way that feels personally significant so they become emotionally invested in our ideas . . . well, we have to temporarily step away from our favorite habits.

Lower Your Standards

We naturally equate excellent work with high standards. And if you are making a machine or a system that doesn't need to interface with humans, that is a good assumption. However, storytellers (and now designers of things that adapt to human experience) have discovered that you have to tolerate a lot of misses in order to design something that feels good and intuitively right to a human listener (user). You will find more on user-experience designers in Chapter 16 to validate this approach, but, for now, it is enough to say that no story will ever work 100 percent of the time.

We are trained to demand proof, to seek excellence (zero defects), and to apply linear analysis to compare and contrast alternatives. These thinking habits keep us from being duped, tricked, or otherwise misled. However, in order to find a story with emotional significance, we must temporarily liberate our search from the burden of proof because there are no reliable measurements for emotions. Think about it: If your spouse says, "If you love me, prove it," what do you do? Buy your spouse a car? Tell your mother to butt out? Or stop buying flowers and start washing the dishes? The answer is subjective: it depends. Important information is often disregarded because, without proof, it is dismissed as too subjective. Storytelling is all about the subjective details that deliver the hard-to-explain state of intuitive knowing, belief, or faith.

Proof does not exist in the subjective frame. In the subjective frame, nothing is true all the time. Actually, sometimes things aren't even true most of the time. Ask someone who is happily married, "Do you love your partner?" and the answer may be "Yes" after a romantic dinner on Friday night. On Saturday morning, however, after missing tee time because his or her "true love" used all the gas and didn't refill the tank, that same happily married someone may be feeling something other than love. The answer to any question about feelings, values, or attitudes is, "It depends."

When I'm facilitating a group, I sound like I think I'm smart—sometimes a little too smart. And I am. I've written several books and have been hired to help important people think through important decisions. So let me share a story about a time I was in Hawaii and saw such a glorious sunset that I got up very early the next morning and went to the same spot waiting to see an equally glorious sunrise. It wasn't until the sun hit my back that I remembered that while the sun goes down in the west, it tends to come up in the east. I can "prove" that I am both smart *and* unbelievably stupid, depending on the situation. Making a human connection is often about telling the good and bad, the smart and stupid, as well as the generous and greedy. In fact, stories that hide all your warts aren't very engaging, but we will get to that later.

When you temporarily embrace the ambiguity of human emotions, it means you can't apply the same standards of consistency to storytelling that you do to rational thinking. Because perfection doesn't exist in human affairs, there are no perfect stories. Forget zero defects. Expect new stories to work about 70 percent of the time—success depends on too many uncontrollable variables. And if you try to control the variables, you come across as coercive or manipulative. In one situation, a technique—for example, a "confident" tone—might improve your story, and yet, in another situation, it might alienate listeners.

No one story will reach 100 percent of your target audience with the exact outcome you desire. For those of us who don't know when to stop chasing perfection, it's good practice to expect a story to feel meaningful to around 70 percent of the people we hope to influence. With 70 percent in mind, I've been able to nudge my expectations down from a higher success rate in order to broaden my experiments and build solid storytelling experience.

Don't Expect a Recipe to Make You a Chef

Increasing your willingness to take risks improves your chances because you tell more stories. It also means you increase your tolerance for imperfection. Think in terms of million-dollar baseball players: a batting average of .300 still means that they strike out twice as often as they hit the ball. Once you expect to miss the mark regularly, you are less likely to ditch storytelling just because a story failed. Like all iterative testing, you tell a story, note the results, and either tell it again or move on to the next story.

While great stories often share certain elements, assembling these elements doesn't necessarily produce a great story. Some people use a recipe approach to storytelling. I even do, at times. My favorite story recipe comes from traditional storyteller Donald Davis, who says that a good story has three parts: Old Normal, Something Happens, New Normal. I can also see the benefit of models from literary or screenwriting sources, such as the eight-point arc[2]: stasis, trigger, the quest, surprise, choice, climax, reversal, and resolution. But I've found that high achievers like you and me are too easily sucked into the illusion that if we just find the right pieces and put them in the right order, we will tell better stories. It's more than that—we must learn to conjure up genuine emotions and relive the story in our imagination in a way that feels significant to us first so our story feels personally significant to others.

Personal Experiences Feel More Real than Facts

The fact that we had to be taught to beware of anecdotal evidence is a testament to the power of specific, tangible, firsthand experiences reported as a story. Anecdotes give us something we can see, hear, taste, touch, and smell—the ultimate criteria our body uses to decide what is worth avoiding or grabbing. Facts are no match for emotions. If we distrust a fact, we discount it. And one off-putting experience or one

---

2. Nigel Watts, *Writing a Novel* (London: Hodder Education, 2006).

hinky detail can be enough to inspire distrust. When you realize that experiences and emotions trump abstractions such as statistics and data, you realize that you are never not telling a story.

This broader definition of *story* encourages you to cast your net wide and test all kinds of experiences that might not fit a recipe or seem immediately relevant but will add depth and emotional connections to your presentation, face-to-face meeting, or telephone conversation. Microsoft's website represents one of their project managers with a photo of him indulging in his hobby, surrounded by wine barrels and sipping a glass of wine. What does wine have to do with project management? For one thing, it makes him a real, multidimensional human being. It also communicates high standards, patience, and discernment. A photo/story that transforms a Microsoft employee into a living, breathing, fellow human with a hobby is reason enough to justify sharing this kind of story-ish detail. Yet because it isn't really an event and there is no real climax to this "story," I worry it might cause you to reject the idea as "not a story." I want you to value your experiments more highly than any recipe.

We crave connection to the natural world and other humans. When we talk about the weather or ask, "How was your trip?" it anchors us in the physical world. The next time someone asks about your trip, experiment by sharing some unique experience such as a conversation you had, an observation, or even a short description of the food, and watch how it animates your exchange. It's refreshing to have our imaginations stimulated. If you are fast on your feet, you might even choose an anecdote that might jump-start the emotions that will best serve your interaction.

Skill sets and recipes work on things that don't think for themselves. Humans *do* think for themselves and vary in so many ways that any attempt at one generalized operator manual or blueprint can make you less effective rather than more effective. Developing your radar to find intense emotions and odd patterns is more valuable than a standardized template.

You can train your brain to "think in story," but first you must unplug your brain from thinking in charts, metrics, and spreadsheets. These kinds of summarizing devices are the culprits that block your imagination from thinking in story. Stories are "predigested," "presummary," and "preconclusion" reports of actual experiences. Imagination is engaged because the experience is still ambiguous in the way that real life is ambiguous. Stories don't squeeze out interpretation; rather, they invite listeners to participate in deciding what a story means. Stories give people freedom to come to their own conclusions. People who reject predigested conclusions might agree with your interpretations after you encourage them to see what you have seen.

Trying to control the way people interpret things puts them on the defensive. It pushes people away from your point of view. By contrast, stories invite people into your perspective and allow them to draw their own conclusions. Stories are more trusting and thus more trustworthy.

The Perfect Story Can Seem Completely Irrelevant

Reciprocity is one of the most reliable predictors of human behavior. We punish those we perceive as free riders. We encourage reciprocal actions from strangers even when it causes us to take irrational risks (with no guarantee of return). This irrational risk (economically) is called trusting someone. Telling a story that reveals some vulnerability is an act of trust that invites a reciprocal act of trust. A tense labor dispute that was at a standstill was dramatically altered when the men (they were all men) shared stories about what it meant to be a father and the values they wanted to pass on to their children. In that particular instance, the emotionally risky stories increased the atmosphere of trust enough that they successfully avoided a strike.

Recently, I've presented storytelling courses at two of the three big military academies. Now that cultural differences, and the Internet, fuel wildly diverse opinions about what is right and how to achieve it, storytelling is a necessary precursor to unified action. The military uses stories to illustrate training, to fuel leadership, and even to sensitize soldiers to the emotional damage that sexual misconduct creates for victims and the military in general. While I had pushback from a few academic historians who absolutely hated the word "subjective," almost every soldier with field experience instinctively understood the role of stories in managing morale, communication, and unified action.

We are getting past the mantra "If you can't measure it, you can't manage it" and learning that if you can't measure it, you have to manage it by paying attention to the stories you tell. Einstein is popularly thought to have said, "Not everything that can be counted counts, and not everything that counts can be counted." When you embed stories as an expected form of communication, you stretch the definition of accountability beyond that which can be controlled or counted. If the company values are regularly reviewed based on the number of true stories illustrating those values, a lack of stories indicates a lack of values in action.

The sheer volume of well-intended measurements we are forced to gather, analyze, and report often distracts us from feeling personal responsibility for creating experiences that engage, inspire, and build trust and respect. Sometimes, the story you need to tell will have nothing to do with the problem as you see it. More than likely, you have had great results solving problems using root cause analysis. When inventory skyrockets, errors increase, or productivity slumps, our immediate response is to perform a root cause analysis. We track data upstream, isolate the beginning of the problem, find the root cause, and fix it. When a problem is perceptual, subjective, or emotionally charged, a root cause analysis can actually make things worse.

In the movie *Saving Private Ryan* (1998), three soldiers were locked in a standoff, each pointing his gun at the head of the next—a serious impasse—when the famously private commander confessed that before the war he was a school teacher. His revelation broke the spell, and they lowered their guns as they turned to attend to his story. A story in Chapter 6 (under the heading "The Time You *Shined*") gives a good example of diverting anger from continued budget cuts by refocusing on a story (a poem actually) that recalled a sense of moral responsibility to take care of those who sacrificed in order to ensure there was a budget in the first place.

Morale is not a function of removing problems. Work is always full of problems. Good morale thrives when a clear sense of personal engagement shrinks unavoidable problems from mountains to tolerable bumps in the road. Unavoidable problems won't go away, but overly negative staff perceptions can. In the subjective world, the solution often has nothing to do with the problem.

Consider addiction. The root cause of alcoholism is drinking too much alcohol. So from a rational perspective, to cure the addiction, you just stop drinking too much. However, this approach doesn't have a terribly high success rate. Instead, Alcoholics Anonymous provides a group experience and invokes a "higher power." Meetings consist almost entirely of shared stories that ultimately create a unified perspective that a higher power will actively support daily improvement.

In 1961, John F. Kennedy shared the Vision story that the United States would soon make it to the moon and back. As a result, he syphoned a lot of negative energy from social unrest and the Bay of Pigs fiasco and channeled it into the space program. Yes, sometimes stories are used to distract investigation into wrongdoing, but that doesn't take away from the fact that a great Vision story can starve negative stories with the promise of better days ahead.

Nonlinear Dynamics

In general, we expect causes and effects to be proportional. One plus one usually equals two. However, the neural network of the brain is not linear. Emotions are not linear. A tiny peep can deliver a strong reaction, and a day spent in meetings can create no reaction at all. Thirty slides do not equal thirty received messages. Good storytellers pay attention to the tiny details that deliver an emotional punch and often edit out important but competing issues to achieve the right emotional impact. It may seem unwise to delete several PowerPoint slides in favor of a story, but the result is often worth it.

In the subjective world of perceptions, little details can make a big difference. Imagine your staff listening intently for three hours as you patiently explain the new IT system that is about to be implemented. Then imagine that as you walk away, you see two staff members rolling their eyes and making "quack-quack" movements with their hands. Which had more of an impact on you: three hours of attention or that one split second? That is an example of nonlinearity—tiny can equal big. Big can also equal tiny. If your child is dying, losing your job because you have run out of vacation time or sick leave is less important than time with your child. Yet the loss of a job for a healthy family can mean disaster. It is all subjective.

With practice, you can apply linear analysis as well as subjective, nonlinear stories to make better decisions. Consider the example of a boss who has four employees and eight hours of overtime to assign.

The linear answer might be the following: eight hours divided by four employees equals two hours of assigned overtime per employee. The nonlinear answer will take into account recent stories that reveal John's kid's birthday is this weekend and that Billy is saving like crazy to buy a motorcycle. So you check with the others and decide together to give Billy all eight hours of overtime. Both answers are perfectly good ways of making a decision yet produce radically different conclusions. In this example, the subjective solution is more stable in terms of staff feelings. Of course, if there is never time to hear personal stories, you will never know this.

When you make a presentation asking for and telling stories that address the emotions surrounding an issue, it may save you from unintended negative results. Put on your objective thinking hat for the numbers, bar charts, and spreadsheets and then take it off and wear your subjective thinking hat for finding and telling stories.

Linear thinkers often get blindsided by emotional responses. They don't have a system for anticipating "irrational" and emotionally charged responses. They think being right is enough. The truth is, facts aren't as powerful as human emotions. Feelings alter facts—at least the perception of facts. If people are mad, sad, or fearful, they discredit facts and attack the credibility of the source. The upside is that when people feel enthusiastic, valued, and inspired, they can attribute more credibility than your facts deserve. Have you seen someone so excited that he or she overstated the case? "We saved $3 million!" when it was in fact $300,000? That's what happens. Perceptions amplify or diminish data.

Being right is only halfway to action. The rest of the way is through perceptions and feelings. Even big data are useless without stories to interpret what all the numbers mean. If people were computers, our data might be predictive, but we can only ever record correlations. It's important to remember that humans will never operate on any reliable cause/effect algorithm, and no matter how much data we gather, we will always need stories to understand and influence the mystery of human desires and fears.

PART 2 **Finding Stories to Tell**

CHAPTER 5

Who-I-Am Stories

THE MOST IMPORTANT story you will ever tell is "Who I am."

Your life is the long version of this story. Everything you have been, have done, haven't done, have dreamed of, will do, will be, and won't be is your story. Your ability to influence people is directly related to what others know or believe about who you are.

This is also called intimacy, and you can help establish intimacy with Who-I-Am stories—that is, telling others something about yourself so they can trust you. People can't trust someone they don't know. If you are so professional and so private that no one really knows you, you are making it twice as hard for others to trust you. A *New York Times/* CBS survey asked, "Of people in general, how many do you think are trustworthy?" On average, people thought about 30 percent of people in general would be trustworthy. Then the survey asked, "Of people *you know*, how many do you think are trustworthy?" The answer? 70 percent. Not only is it statistically impossible for these beliefs to be accurate, but the findings further demonstrate the irrational, nonlinear dynamics of trust. If I feel I know you personally, I attribute twice as much trustworthiness to you. If you are a stranger, I give you a 30 percent chance of being trustworthy. Familiarity builds a bridge between you and your listener so your information can get to them.

Often, those we need to influence don't know us very well, so they can't trust us. A good Who-I-Am story is like increasing the bandwidth between you and your listeners, thus increasing the amount of information your listeners are ready to receive.

It makes sense that most people would prefer not to trust. Treating others as untrustworthy makes life easier. For our primitive ancestors, assuming the worst-case scenario was a survival mechanism, and it still is. We tend to fill in the blanks with cautionary tales. Think about it. Do you make up a good story when your boss says, "I need to see you in my office in five minutes?" "Hey, I bet I'm gonna get a raise!" Or do you tend to construct stories along the lines of, "Oh no, what went wrong now?"

So people make up stories (without realizing it) that paint us as ambitious, greedy, inexperienced, or stupid: anything that justifies not listening. Listening—really listening—might force us to question our current beliefs, change direction, or risk the complication of caring.

Your job is to break through the worst-case-scenario stories so people can see, at a deeper level, who you really are beneath the surface. You need to tell a good story about who you are in order to gain the trust of others. Your first step in developing your Who-I-Am story is to answer these questions: Who are you? What makes you special? What earns you the right to influence? Everyone has gifts. What are yours? Are you compassionate, reliable, honest, or diplomatic? (These four qualities do not usually define the same person.) What is it in you that earns you the right to influence others?

Exercise: Who Are You?

What qualities do you have that earn you the right to influence others? List the qualities that "earn you the right to influence" (e.g., trustworthy, passionate, responsible, creative, compassionate, honest, diplomatic). People want evidence that you have these qualities. Make it personal. Trust is always a personal decision.

After you have a list, start looking for stories that demonstrate these qualities in a visceral way. Give your listeners an experiential sample of them so they can decide from their personal experiences that you are trustworthy.

Here are examples of Who-I-Am stories from the four buckets I described in Chapter 3. As you read each one, take a few minutes to jot down ideas for stories you might develop for telling.

A Time You *Shined*

I get energy when I see how sharing a story can make people feel more alive, live better, and take opportunities they couldn't even see before.

I do a lot of *pro bono* work, and as part of that, a friend and I designed a process called PhotoStory. We borrowed this method from Caroline Wang's photovoice, a storytelling tool that originated when Wang gave disposable cameras to poor women in China so they could communicate their needs even though they did not speak English. It turned out to be more powerful than a simple needs-analysis tool. The pictures traveled and told the women's stories at a very personal level. We adapted Wang's photo ideas and added storytelling to do some action research with a community in Houston that was so poor and dangerous that even pizza delivery drivers refused to go there.

We asked people to use the cameras to tell their stories and share them with a group. Participants said telling the stories of their environment in this way motivated them to take action to improve their lives. They said, "It opened our eyes" and moved them into an "I'm going to do something" mode.

The process opened one woman's eyes enough for her to make big changes. She originally nodded off to sleep in meetings because she had a morphine pump that treated terrible pain from a botched cancer treatment on her spine. She had given up. Yet I saw her three years later, and she had removed the morphine pump and was wide awake. She contacted service agencies and rattled the cages of people who weren't doing their jobs. She got a computer and started a community health program.

Think about it. When did you stick your neck out? Was there a time when you decided to step out on a limb? If so, the experience would make a great Who-I-Am story.

A Time You *Blew It*

When I first started my consulting business, I landed a very big client. I was still testing ideas, but I didn't want to seem inexperienced. I confess that I had one of those answering machine messages that said, "We can't come to the phone right now" as if I had a whole staff there. I was working out of my house. "We" could only mean me or my dog, Larry. He sure as heck wasn't going to answer the phone, even if he'd had opposing thumbs.

Back to the client. I had a process that I had used many times, which I sold to Mark, the vice president of services. He asked me if I could adapt the process to accommodate 70 people. I looked him straight in the eye and said, "Sure." What I didn't explain was that I'd never done this process with more than 20 people. Basically, the process was to gather and compile customer comments (piece of cake) and then hand out verbatim customer comments for the team to analyze. I knew they'd value their own conclusions more than a research company's summary and recommendations. But 70 people agreeing on their interpretations? I designed logistical aids. Participants were to cut out the most important comments and collectively assemble them on the walls with sticky notes in a way that simultaneously made sense and demonstrated the frequency of recurrence. I assigned different-colored highlighters to mean different things. I thought I had it covered.

About halfway through, I looked around and one group had stolen all the highlighters to make a tower. Paper was everywhere. It was chaos. Mark came over and stood beside me, rocking once front to back on the balls of his feet.

He asked, "You've never done this before, have you?"

I said, "Nope."

He nodded. "Didn't think so."

Then he smiled, handed me a bottle of water, and said, "Thought you might be thirsty," and walked away.

Bless his heart. I'll always remember his kindness. The process wasn't a total disaster. We did get more cohesive action out of those people. But never again! I had my own little Scarlet O'Hara moment with my fist in the air, "So help me God, I will never again overpromise or underdeliver." It's better for everyone that way.

Think of a time when you really blew it or a time when you acted out of character. Counterintuitively, people will more readily believe you understand the value of a specific quality when they see how you talk about failing your own standards.

A Mentor

This story is about a mentor I've never met. His name is Antanas Mockus, a past mayor of Bogotá. A friend from Colombia told me about the traffic problems they were having in Bogotá. The only people that owned cars were rich, and they thought traffic rules were suggestions. They ran red lights or nudged through pedestrian crossings, and people were getting killed.

Now imagine what you or I would do to solve this problem. Better enforcement? Stiffer penalties? Not Antanas Mockus. He hired mimes—I'm not making this up. He hired mimes to monitor the pedestrian crossings and other risky areas. The mimes called attention to any motorist disobeying the rules. They would wag their fingers, signal stop, or call pedestrians over to help train a driver to follow the rules. And guess what? Pedestrian deaths dropped by more than half.

After visiting Bogotá, I e-mailed a copy of the magazine article I wrote to a guy who worked for the administration, Juan Uribe, and he e-mailed me back: "The way you write the story says that the mimes trained the drivers to obey rules. No, the mimes trained the pedestrians that they had rights."

Oh yeah, big difference. That's the kind of work I want to do in the world.

Who taught you what was truly important in this world? It might have been a parent, grandparent, or maybe even a teacher, scout leader, or old boss. When you tell a story that paints a loving portrait of your mentor and demonstrates that you paid close attention to his or her actions, you reveal as much about yourself as about the person in your story.

A Book, Movie, or Current Event

When I first developed a training course on storytelling, I used clips from the movie *Amistad* (1997). Many of us, at one time or another, have faced injustice so great that our task has felt impossible. For me, this movie is a good example of trying to achieve the impossible and succeeding.

In the film *Amistad*, 44 West Africans who had been snatched from their homes, chained, starved, and beaten took control of their captors' ship but were apprehended trying to get home and sent to the United States. Can you imagine being their lawyer? Trying to get justice for black men and women in a country where slavery is legal and where talk of slavery threatens to spark a civil war? President Martin Van Buren is up for reelection and would rather not rush into a civil war. You are speaking to a jury of 12 white guys on behalf of 44 black men and women who don't speak a word of English. That's what I call trying to achieve the impossible.

But they won. How? In the movie, a grumpy former president, John Quincy Adams, refuses to formally help but gives a frustrated abolitionist a hint: "In a court of law, I've found that whoever tells the best story wins." So they found a translator, learned a firsthand account of what happened, and retold their story in a way that was so compelling it outlasted four overturned verdicts. It even convinced a handpicked judge to find them innocent, even though it would be suicide for his career. Their story was so emotionally powerful that no one who heard it could deny them the justice they deserved.

Think about your favorite movies. I bet if you watch one of them again, you will find that the scenes that move you include tests of the qualities you personally value. A character may shine or blow it. The events may illustrate the consequences of losing the quality. The scenes that stick in your mind, stick in your mind for a reason.

CHAPTER 6

Why-I-Am-Here Stories

I **N A WORKSHOP** I was conducting, a participant told a story about toying with the idea of lying to a police officer. He started his story with the dreaded phrase, "Sir, do you know how fast you were going?" and then described looking in his rearview mirror at his four-year-old daughter's eyes. He had heard himself only minutes ago reassuring her mommy, "Relax, I'm only going 10 miles over the speed limit."

Seeing his daughter, he resisted the urge to lie and say, "No." His story left me with the impression that he was essentially a truth teller, even when sorely tempted to tell a lie. His desire to be a good dad earned points with me and, judging by the comments, with the rest of the group. Everyone feels an urge to lie at some point. Someone with enough self-awareness and integrity to admit to that urge publicly is more trustworthy than someone who hides that flaw. His story was a good enough answer to my implicit question, "Why are you here?" He told me, "I'm here to do the right thing even when I don't want to." Once I know this, I'm ready to listen to the ideas he has to share.

Telling Others What's in It for You

This guy answered the question that anyone who listens to you is going to ask: "What's in it for you?" Yes, you and I were taught in Marketing and Sales 101 that answering your listener's WIIFM—"What's In It For Me?"—should be first. And yes, people certainly need to know what's in it for them. However, I've noticed (and you may also have noticed) that people don't relax and listen to what is in it for them until they are satisfied they know what's in it for you.

No one wants to feel conned. Most people assume if you have taken time, effort, and money to ask them to do something, you are getting something out of it. There is an internal sense of fairness that judges the ratio of what you get out of this exchange in comparison to what they get. They don't mind that you get paid to "sell" ideas or products. If you seek no money or personal advantage out of the deal, they will, with evidence, buy into altruism.

Even when people know they will get exactly what they want, they scan the deal for any evidence that you might be using them in some way. Any sniff of exploitation from a transaction can be enough for a person to pull the plug, even if it costs them.

Simulations in experimental economics, such as investment games and public good games, reveal that fairness and reciprocity often matter more than utility. If an offer feels exploitative, people prefer to take nothing and will even pay their own money to punish a "free rider." People don't like users.

The stories of shifty accounting scams from Enron, Bernie Madoff, Countrywide, and Wall Street have further increased the demand for proof that you will operate with integrity and transparency. The burden is on you, then, to share a positive story about the benefits you reap if listeners heed your call to action.

People tend to choose to buy from those who are motivated by a love of the product over those who are only in it for the money. It is natural for people to assume we are selling something—that we are up to some sort of self-serving sneakiness that will benefit us more than it benefits them. And they don't want or need some idea that will increase the number of things they have to do today. This is perfectly normal. Suspicion is a good defense against being duped.

Only a strong connection to your positive intent can keep suspicion from clouding your message or discrediting your data. When you prove your positive intent by sharing a story of a past client success that eclipsed your own sacrifice or a story of joyfully watching your client discover a new idea, curiosity can overcome suspicion.

Here are examples of Why-I-Am-Here stories from all four buckets. Read each one, and immediately take a few minutes to jot down ideas of stories you might develop for yourself. After you have examined "why" you do what you do, start looking for stories that demonstrate the benefits you seek to project.

Exercise: Why You Are Here

Think about the last time someone said "thank you" for a job well done. Find the stories that will let your listeners see that you really are there for the right reasons. If you make a timeline of your proudest moments, you will likely find a great Why-I-Am-Here story.

A Time You *Shined*

I was once hired by a group of military decision makers housed in the Pentagon to help facilitate a budget meeting. Their budgets had been cut about 15 percent every year for the last three years. At each annual budget meeting after the cuts, the group left with action plans and good intentions to innovate and, if absolutely necessary, cut services in proportion to budget cuts. For three years, these decisions were overturned, ignored, or overcome by critical events. The group had not succeeded in making any substantial cuts to accommodate dwindling resources. They were still trying to provide all the services they had provided three years ago with fewer and fewer resources. They were squeezed so tight that everyone was frustrated and some were downright angry. Blame was starting to seep into e-mails, and the group was poised for a showdown. Budget meetings are typically considered a battleground anyway, so the atmosphere was tense, suspicious, and cynical.

So I used poetry to change the story they might be telling themselves about why they were there (to battle for the budget) and why I was there (to referee the bloodbath). I began, "We need to talk about feelings before we get to the numbers." I talked really fast before they could kick me out. "I want to draw your attention to the feeling state that wins a war, and then we will examine the feeling state that helps you make good decisions about allocating resources."

"Let's examine the feeling state that wins a war first," I said. "I'd like to recite part of a speech from Shakespeare's *Henry V*":

> *Once more unto the breach, dear friends, once more;*
> *Or close the wall up with our English dead.*
> *In peace there's nothing so becomes a man*
> *As modest stillness and humility:*
> *But when the blast of war blows in our ears,*
> *Then imitate the action of the tiger;*
> *Stiffen the sinews, summon up the blood,*
> *Disguise fair nature with hard-favour'd rage.*
>   *(*Henry V, *3.1:1–8)*

By the time I finished, they were hulked into bodybuilder poses doing the Tim Allen grunt, "H-o-o-Ho-o-Ho-o." I said, "This is how you work up a group to win a war with speed and aggression. This emotional state evokes specific behaviors, such as surprise attacks, diversion, and secrecy. But we aren't here to fight a war. We are here to make sober, calm budget decisions."

"This next poem describes the emotional state from which we can make wise, more considered decisions. This emotional state inspires very different behaviors."

Then I read from Billy Rose's poem "The Unknown
Soldier":[3]

"I am the Unknown Soldier,"
The spirit voice began,
"And I think I have the right
To ask some questions man to man.

"Are my buddies taken care of?
Was their victory so sweet?
Is that big reward you offered
Selling pencils on the street?

"Did they really win the freedom
They battled to achieve?
Do you still respect that Croix de Guerre
Above that empty sleeve?"

I asked them, "Can you feel the difference?"
You could have heard a pin drop.

"Imagine the face of a person you know who died
on the battlefield. If that man or woman could speak
from the grave right now, what would they ask you to
remember? What would they tell you to forget?"

These two poems changed the emotional climate
in the room by changing the context of the task from
a small picture of battling for money to the bigger

---

3.   Billy Rose, "The Unknown Soldier," *The Best Loved Poems of the American People.* Ed. Hazel Felleman (Garden City, New York: Doubleday,
1936), pp. 428–429.

picture of using this meeting as an opportunity for us to repay the men and women who sacrifice their lives for our country. Frustration turned to courage, anger to resolve, and arrogance to humility. The conversations they had and the decisions they made were much more collaborative and more firmly grounded. By reciting these poems, I let them see (and judge) my feelings of gratitude for soldiers' sacrifices and my compassion for the frustrations they faced. I was there to facilitate, but I was driven by gratitude and compassion rather than ego, control needs, or other dynamics that drive some facilitators to referee instead of facilitate. By demonstrating faith that they could referee themselves, I redefined my role as well.

We all have some idea of "doing the right thing for the right reasons." Think back to a time when you felt like you did the right thing for the right reasons. Or even the "wrong thing" for the right reasons.

Life is complex, and these kinds of stories aren't often told because it feels risky to discuss moral judgments that could be contrary to a listener's personal opinions. Morals seem old fashioned. However, no one wants to collaborate with someone devoid of a moral compass, so sharing a story about why you are here anchors trust with a tangible demonstration that you have a moral compass—even if it isn't exactly the same as his or hers. Because the world changes just about every day, people crave some kind of "evidence" that you won't exploit unpredictable ambiguities or unforeseen events by taking more than your fair share. Don't be discouraged that it is impossible to define right or wrong. Just tell a story that illustrates how you previously did your dead-level best to do right and avoid wrong so your listeners can relax a bit.

In general, increasing the level of risk you feel when revealing your Why-I-Am-Here story makes it more surprising—and thus more memorable to your audience. Screenwriter Robert McKee points out that an obvious choice is boring. Choosing between two bad options and two good options is much more interesting. I'm not sure what we'd call this emotional state, but, such as in the title of one of my favorite Gillian Welch songs, we have all experienced the state of "I wanna do right, but not right now." Tell a story that prompts a second take from original assumptions.

A Time You *Blew It*

One of my all-time favorite self-disclosure stories was told by a very dignified senior partner of a global accounting and consulting firm. They hired me to teach storytelling to increase clients' feelings of trust toward their firm. When the time came to share stories in a room of 150 partners, not one person was willing to risk going first—which tells you a bit about trust *inside* that firm. They were forever competing with each other for resources and assignments. After a long wait, one of the most respected and powerful men in the room stood and walked to the front.

He said, "I had a really good day last month. My team was playing, and I was there watching from the 50-yard line. We won the game. I was a happy man. I went back to my hotel room. I ordered a cheeseburger, fries, and two beers. After room service delivered it, in order to properly enjoy my feast, I stripped down to my tighty-whities, and I ate every bit of it." His smile was huge.

"Lordy, I was a happy man. Until I went to set my tray outside, and the napkin caught the glass, which tipped off the tray. When I reached to catch it, I heard the click."

"I guess I should've realized there would be people on the elevator. But when it opened, I did a little left-right-left look before I decided to hide behind a nearby palm tree."

"After that, I punched the button and hid until I finally got an empty elevator. On my way down, I realized I would soon have another problem." He paused. "I decided speed would be my friend, so I streaked across the lobby. Halfway across, I heard someone at the desk yell out, 'What number?' I told them, grabbed my new card key, ran back."

"When I was safe in my room, out of breath from my adventure, the phone rang. I puffed out, 'Hello?' This sweet voice said, 'Sir, we just wanted you to know, if this ever happens again, we have phones on every floor.'"

The group was still laughing when he sat down.

His story told the group, "I'm here to learn and have fun. This isn't a competition, and I'm willing to embarrass myself to learn." Once they heard his story almost everyone else decided that was why they were there as well, and the stories flowed.

Think about a time you caved in and regretted your action. Or perhaps there was a situation where you made a mistake, could have hidden it, but didn't.

Big mistakes make fabulous stories as long as we aren't telling about unfinished issues. This is not the place to purge old shame and clean out an old skeleton for the first time. However, if we are emotionally finished with an issue and have tested the skeleton for reactions, it's a great time to turn a mistake into a good story. When you tell a *mea culpa* story about your own mistakes, it cheats your adversaries of the opportunity to discredit your intentions, and the story polishes your reputation for transparency at the same time.

A Mentor

One of my mentors was Dr. Jim Farr. He always said, "A difference to be a difference must make a difference." By 1993, when I first met him, Jim had been a practicing psychologist for 45 years and had been teaching leadership for 25 years. He was 75 at the time: loving, compassionate, and brilliant, rolled up into one grumpy package. After an influx of capital, I was one of six new recruits learning how to facilitate the "Self-Awareness Workshops" that were the backbone of his firm's successful leadership training series.

Jim didn't tiptoe around the truth. He told it like it was. Those of us who worked for him teased that he was "lovingly abusive." He could work you over, that's for sure. Jim was an in aikido master, the martial art dedicated to avoiding a fight or ending a fight quickly with the least effort. In aikido, when someone comes after you, the idea is to tap into his momentum and turn his attack into a little face time with the floor. Jim did this mentally as well as physically. I was taking aikido lessons to learn how to do it as well, but mostly I learned how to roll when I hit the ground.

One day in a staff meeting, Jim told me I wasted too much energy struggling against the flow. I leaned toward a perfectionist style and was often defensive when I got feedback from the other recruits. Basically, I had been driving everyone nuts. He stood up, motioned for me to stand next to him, and said, "Throw me a punch." I stuck my fist out in my best impression of a punch, and two seconds later, I was on the floor. I was a fit 32 years old, and he was 75. Then he did it again in slow motion. I threw the punch; instead of punching me back, he took my "offered" fist and pulled me toward him, stepping left. He kept pulling until my body followed the momentum started when I punched. I was on the floor again.

He asked, "Now do you get it?"

I'll never forget him or that moment.

He taught me that what I interpreted as a punch was not always an "attack" that must be returned. It can also be an invitation to turn in that person's direction, to see what they see. At that point, I can stop and look or keep the momentum swinging back around to my point of view. It doesn't work all the time, but at least I learned that I can choose from a variety of responses when I feel criticized. In fact, I don't have to respond at all until after I see the situation from their point of view. I'm here to learn, not debate.

People rarely have long conversations about why we are here, but if you reflect on it, you will find one or two people who inspired you by their example. What person comes to your mind when you think about why you are here?

A Book, Movie, or Current Event

A manager of a large retail company found himself with really bad numbers to report at the next sales meeting of more than 2,000 sales staff members. It was 2002, and September 11, 2001, had made a real dent in that year's performance. They had done the best they could, but they had still failed to meet their goals.

The manager chose to reframe, facing that "failure" as heroic rather than weak by using a scene from the film *The Matrix* (1999). In this great movie about choices, an underground operative has powerful information that will change the neophyte from an amateur into a warrior for justice. Accepting the responsibilities of knowing this information takes courage. It is a tough road. Morpheus wants Neo to understand that knowledge and wisdom can be a bitter pill to swallow, and he offers Neo a choice between a red pill or a blue pill.

The manager retells the scene.

Morpheus (with a blue pill in his hand): "You take the blue pill and the story ends. You wake up in your bed and believe whatever you want to believe. (A red pill is now shown in his other hand.) You take the red pill and I show you how deep the rabbit-hole goes."

Neo thinks long and hard. He starts to reach for the red pill.

Morpheus: "Remember, all I am offering is the truth, nothing more."

The manager continued with his address. "So that's all I've got. Denial or a positive spin would be easier. We have some tough decisions to make. But I'd rather deal with the truth. What about you? Do you want the red pill, the truth, or do you want me to blow blue smoke?"

Of course, the entire auditorium erupted in chants of "Red Pill! Red Pill!" This story transformed him from coming across as a critical parent with bad news to becoming the magician and mentor ready to help the real heroes (his audience) seek out truth and understanding—good storytelling.

Again, with a movie, the special effects and talent are already there, all you need to do is describe a scene and bring it back to life. I like books even more. John Steinbeck is one of my favorite authors because he shows how the contrast between good and bad makes a story more realistic. Steinbeck includes both what is good and what is terrible about human nature without making me want to cut my wrists. A scene from Steinbeck brings authenticity that never smacks of over-optimistic, upbeat perkiness. Borrowing "old soul" wisdom from this kind of gritty realism lends *gravitas* and credibility to your words.

Is there one book or movie that exemplifies the big "why" for you? It may have nothing to do with the particular situation, but if it inspired you to be a better person, then it is a good story. Any movie or book that inspires you can inspire others.

CHAPTER 7

Teaching Stories

AT ITS BEST, a Teaching story transports listeners into an experience that empowers them to emotionally feel as well as hear, see, taste, touch, and smell an excellent performance or the unforgettable consequences of a poor performance. It demonstrates how new behaviors create new results. It is a no-risk demonstration: a trial by imagination.

Charles Dickens's novels are full of Teaching stories. In *A Christmas Carol*, Dickens shows us how Teaching stories work. Scrooge's ghosts take Scrooge on Teaching-story tours. Each ghost tells a different Teaching story, allowing Scrooge to emotionally and mentally experience the consequences of not changing his behavior.

> **STORY ONE:** In your past, you delayed your marriage to make more money and lost Belle, your one true love.

> **STORY TWO:** Your obsession with money keeps the Cratchit family in poverty.

STORY THREE: If you continue, this obsession with money will kill the Cratchits' son, and you will die alone and miserable.

It was a three-story transformation delivered in one night. Teaching stories travel in time and perspective to deliver simulated experiences. They enable us to take a trial run at doing the right or smart thing in a difficult situation. Experiences delivered in story form are far more effective than scolding or preaching. My good friend Pam McGrath, a minister, preached a sermon on evangelism that began with a story of her own experience in a grocery-store checkout line that demonstrates how even a simple story can transform an experience. She told it like this:

> A woman and her children are grocery shopping after work on Friday. The store is fraught with danger: giant cereal boxes, bags of candy, oversized bottles of pop. The woman is at wit's end. Just as she finally makes her way to the head of a cashier's line, the checkout machine runs out of tape. She impatiently taps her foot while the kids grab things from the confined area. The checkout girl is rushing. Everyone in the line behind her sighs. Then the woman notices the checkout girl has on a cross like her mom used to wear.
>
> She says, "Nice cross."
>
> The checkout girl stops and looks into her eyes. They smile.
>
> She continues, "My mother used to have one like that."
>
> The checkout girl says, "My mom gave me this one."

They both breathe and smile. Two humans take the opportunity to connect and feel human again.

Pam's story teaches that showing kindness and giving the gift of human attention are better ways to share her church's religious message than passing out brochures. I can't help but compare this story to the mindless attempt of some companies to mandate a cheerful and helpful attitude from grocery-store clerks by giving them a scripted greeting. I feel sorry for a clerk forced to ask, "Did you find everything you need?" Increased clarity in this case actually degrades customer relations. What if I said no? Should the five people behind me wait while I explain, "As a matter of fact, no. I did not find the gnocchi." Not only is this question badly timed, but the person asking it can't really help if the answer is no. A boss who forces the staff to follow this sort of script tells the story that management lacks faith in the staff's ability to greet customers and tend to customer needs, and this lack of faith is reciprocated when a clerk becomes mechanically polite but inattentive. Teaching stories that narrate a variety of responses would be more engaging and encourage the kind of attention to detail that is, in itself, an act of kindness.

Some Teaching stories rewind a past action so you can view it from another perspective. For instance, if you were training a new caregiver at a nursing home, it would be wonderful if you could put that strong twenty-four-year-old person into an eighty-seven-year-old body for one day so he or she can feel the vibrations of Parkinson's disease distort his or her ability to walk or sit still. He or she could feel what it is like to be dependent and how belittling it feels to have someone say, "And how are we today?" in that singsong voice normally reserved for toddlers. Such a personal experience would stay with him or her forever. But we can't switch bodies, so the next best thing is to bring life-altering experiences to those who can benefit from Teaching stories.

I am not suggesting you use stories for everything. We need rules, policies, and even scripts to protect critical systems, life-or-death situations, and times when accuracy is more important than empathy. Many worst-case-scenario-derived rules and procedures save lives. Hospital staff need clarity for technical issues such as attaching IVs. However, following policy is not likely to build a nurse's skill in calming a frightened patient. And even technical tasks are reinforced by stories that engrave the importance of inflexible perfection on a trainee by delivering a visceral experience of a worst-case scenario.

One caveat for using stories to teach: remember, it only works about 70 percent of the time. When you inspire and encourage people to think for themselves, they are more actively engaged and pay better attention. However, at times, their interpretation will not be what you expected. That's the price you pay for creative engagement. On the other hand, their unexpected interpretation may be even better than what you had in mind.

Exercise: Share a Pet Peeve

Now it's time to think of a skill you want to teach. Why not start with a pet peeve you have with a task that is, in your opinion, poorly done? If you have a pet peeve over it, you've probably accumulated some negative assumptions and emotional baggage that could fracture your ability to tell a Teaching story without sounding judgmental. Step back and review the task you feel needs improvement. Consider it from the other person's point of view. What experience could you share in story form that might change his or her approach? Can you find a story about a significant emotional event he or she might otherwise never witness and use it as a Teaching story?

Here are four Teaching stories from our four buckets to get your juices flowing with ideas.

A Time You *Shined*

There are many courses on cultural sensitivity. If you had enough time to get a master's degree or a Ph.D. in cultural differences, you could list thousands of specific ways to offend people in different cultures: showing the soles of your feet in an Arab country or pointing with your index finger in India. Yet ultimately the most important skill to learn is constant sensitivity to interpretations that don't match your expectations.

A story I heard by a young lady named Cindy, recently returned from two years in the Peace Corps, makes this point with humor. She told of being stationed in the Philippines. Her tour of duty began with a week living with a local resident. She had expected her home stay to be prearranged and structured, similar to traveling with the church choir back home. Instead, she and her new Peace Corps buddies were "sort of auctioned off" to families who picked them from the line where they stood.

Individuals or families picked out the volunteer they wanted and led them out the door. The middle-aged woman who selected Cindy did not speak English. Cindy didn't speak

Tagalog. Her advisor assured her this was OK, and she should follow the woman and come back in a week. So she did.

This is her story:

> She took me farther and farther away from clean streets and houses with walls. The regular houses stopped, and in their place were tarps on frames, lean-tos, and cardboard boxes. Finally, we arrived at a lean-to right next to the town dump. There were no walls. The floor was the dirt on the ground. I wasn't disgusted so much as, well . . . I was scared.
>
> There were bugs everywhere. But I put on a brave face, and I helped where I could. We went to get some food and prepared it on an outdoor fire. We ate dinner. I didn't eat much. I didn't feel so good.
>
> It got dark. I needed to go to the bathroom but didn't see a bathroom. I didn't see a latrine. I mean I wasn't looking for a tiled floor or a door that said "Ladies." I knew the facilities would be basic, but I didn't expect them to be invisible. I tried to watch to see what others did, but I still didn't know where in the world they went when they needed to "go," and I couldn't ask because I didn't speak the language.
>
> Finally, it got urgent. I needed to go, so I had to mime to the lady who was my host. I used the knock-kneed, bouncing-up-and-down motion that is an international symbol of "I need to go." She laughed and laughed, and then she showed me in mime that they did number one in a corner nearby in the dirt. Then she began to mime how to handle number two. She took a plastic grocery bag and indicated that I should use the

bag as a toilet, and she handed me the bag. But I was still confused. What would I do with the bag when I was done? She could see my confusion and smiled, took the bag, pretended to swing the bag over her head like a shot put, and hurled it off in the direction of the dump, speaking the only two English words I heard the entire week: "Flying Saucer!"

Her story cracked us up. There were 250 people in the room, and the phrase "flying saucer" became a code for learning to let go and adapt. This story is specific to the Philippines and yet is useful to any group facing cultural differences.

A Time You *Blew It*

I was inspired by a story in the *New York Times* written nine months after the 2003 space shuttle *Columbia* disaster in which all crew members died. You know part of the story already:

When the *Columbia* took off, a piece of foam broke off the wing and, without it, the craft burned up on reentry over Texas on February 1, 2003. With the 20/20 hindsight of an in-depth investigation, it was discovered that the data that predicted this disaster were available but were buried deep inside a PowerPoint slide. Edward Tufte, a professor from Yale who specializes in the visual presentation of data, analyzed the slide. The information was in the last line of a 19-line slide and read: "Flight condition is significantly outside test database, volume of ramp is 1920 cu. in. vs. 3 cu. in. for test."

This was a situation of poor visual storytelling. Much has been made of how visually insignificant this "significantly" relevant data appeared to be in relation to the other information on that slide. But more important, this story highlights how words on a screen rarely deliver enough context to interpret the data's meaning in terms of human life. Storytelling is about attracting attention to what is most important or building perspective that makes some data more meaningful than the rest.

The data were there. The piece that broke off in the test was hundreds of times larger than anything they'd ever tested to be safe. But it was out of context. Could lives have been saved with a metaphor such as "Similar to losing the door panel of your car?" Did PowerPoint kill those people? No. Ted Simons, editor of online magazine *Presentations*, coined the headline, "PowerPoint doesn't kill presentations, people do." My main concern is that PowerPoint lets you think you communicated when you didn't.

There was a cartoon in the *New Yorker*—a scene from Hell's human resources headquarters—where a recruiter for Hell is interviewing a new torturer. The recruiter leans back from his desk, looks at the prospect, and asks, "That's all fine and good, but do you know PowerPoint?"

A Mentor

People often complain about a lack of civility. One hospital group I work with launched an initiative to improve civility, and they discovered it also improved patient safety performance. Incivility operates like a contagious virus. When someone treats an employee badly, he or she is likely to pass it on to a customer or patient who is then rude in return. It's a terrible spiral. We parrot the words, "The customer is always right," but that's not always true. Employees can end up feeling abused, because no one ever acknowledges how hard it is to be nice to a mean client or an angry and abusive patient.

Here's a story from a woman in one of my classes. She told it without a trace of bitterness or self-pity and redefined the alternatives to thinking like a victim.

> I was the ugly girl in high school. As an adult, I now know that every class has one. Your class had an "ugly girl." So that was me. I was the one with cooties in grade school; the freak who was picked last in gym; and in high school, there was a group of boys who made my life a living hell. No matter where I hid, they'd find me. After school, I'd hang back or find a bench far away from the rest of the kids. I waited on my own for my mother to pick me up. I was as invisible as I could be.
>
> Anyway, those boys would eventually find me, no matter where I hid. When they found me, they'd start to play their favorite game. One of them would sit beside me, put his arm around me, and they'd all laugh as he'd pretend to ask me out on a date, beg me for a kiss. I would try not to cry, but my chin would start to quiver. The more I cried, the more they laughed. This went on for most of a year. Then one day, I have *no* idea what came over me, one of these boys had his arm around me, taunting me, and something—not really me, but *something*—lifted my left arm and draped it right back over this boy's

shoulder and gave him a squeeze. Then my brain kicked in, and I actually winked at him. Now the other boys weren't laughing at me anymore, they were laughing at him. I air kissed him, and I started to laugh, too. I wish you could've seen his face; it was pretty funny.

From that day on things were different. Sure, they still teased me, but I never again let myself feel so devastated. I had power, and I used it.

It is an old but excellent strategy: find someone who is successful and copy him or her. I still think of this woman as a role model. Retelling a story about the habits, mannerisms, and daily goals of successful people puts you one step closer to learning (and teaching others) how to recreate their results. Find people who have the skills you want. Study their stories, and tell their stories. We tend to teach what we need to learn, and I can't think of a better way to do it.

A Book, Movie, or Current Event

A friend of mine is a therapist. To keep his license, he must constantly earn education credits by attending courses on the latest developments in mental health. He frequently attends free trainings produced by the pharmaceutical industry to keep abreast of the medications they offer and to fulfill his licensing requirements. Sometimes I like to go too, if there is an opportunity to learn more about neuroscience, emotions, and mental health.

The presenters vary considerably in quality. They are all smart. Most have M.D. or Ph.D. degrees, but only a few are interesting to listen to. One psychiatrist speaker captured everyone's attention when he narrated a story from a movie. He was in the middle of a deck of PowerPoint slides, with graphs of results from experiments in treating manic depression, and I could feel my eyes glazing over as I tried to deal with unfamiliar words such as *lamotrigine* and *carbamazepine*. I woke up when I heard him say,

> We forget how inexact this science is. You know, it's only 60 years since we discovered lithium. John Cade, the Australian who discovered the use of lithium for mania in 1947, is the subject of a new movie. At the time, everyone else used electric shock or lobotomies. John Cade started wondering if manic behavior might be a result of too much of something. What if the body was intoxicating itself with some internally produced stimulant? He was treating 10 manic patients at a nearby institution, so he started collecting their urine and feeding it to guinea pigs to see if that "too much of something" might turn their behavior manic, too. Nothing happened, so he decided to inject the guinea pigs with the urine. In order to do that he needed some kind of salt combination to act as the base fluid. Through trial and error, he discovered that lithium carbonate worked best.
>
> However, when he injected the guinea pigs, the mixture had a strong sedating effect—the very opposite of his theory. He was so curious that he tried it on himself to see if it was safe enough to try it on a patient.
>
> He knew which patient he wanted to treat first: a terribly manic man who was bouncing off the walls. This man's mania was so bad that he had lost his job and was institutionalized. Almost immediately after the

injection, the man was "more settled, tidier, able to pay attention and to control his impulses." After two weeks of injections, the man was able to leave the institution and go back to work. It was a miracle.

John Cade discovered the miracle 50 years ago, and *we still don't know why it works.*

The psychiatrist then paused and looked up at his graphs in silence. You can bet we hung on every word he had to say next about his research. His narrative reintroduced enough ambiguity to reactivate curiosity and discussion.

There aren't many human issues that haven't been addressed in one way or another by a movie. The classic *To Kill a Mockingbird* (1962) can stand up to high-school students even today. It is still engaging enough to induce introspection about racism, integrity, humility, and stereotyping.

When I love a scene in a movie, I try to take notes in case an application arises someday. I no longer feel concerned about when and where I will use the story because if it was powerful enough to stop me in my tracks, then I'm confident the opportunity will arise.

CHAPTER 8
Vision Stories

WHEN I WAS a kid, my mother taught me table manners by suggesting I'd need them, "In case the queen ever invites you to tea." I'm over fifty, and so far I've received no royal invitations, but I do have lovely table manners.

The queen's tea party was my mother's version of a Vision story. When I was eight, using a short fork for salad seemed ridiculous without my mother's "You'll thank me someday" story about my future self barely avoiding public humiliation at a royal tea party. We can always use a good Vision story to help develop moral character and delayed gratification, no matter how old we are.

Unpleasant chores, training, routine maintenance, and disruptive changes in procedure rarely offer much immediate gratification. Frustration experienced in the here and now is like an advance payment against some payoff we hope to reap in the future. A good Vision story makes your promise for future payoffs tangible enough to feel realistic. When you make a vision come alive with carefully crafted images, sounds, smells, tastes, and feelings, you eclipse the burden of today with tomorrow's reward. Overwhelming obstacles shrink to bearable frustrations that are achievable and worth the effort.

A Vision story raises your gaze from current difficulties, complexity, and ambiguity to see a future worth the effort of resisting daily temptations to change direction, give up, compromise, or seek distractions. Without a visceral and easily remembered vision, it is easy to forget who we are and why we are here.

A Vision story builds a sensory, imagined future, just like a bright, shiny bicycle in a store window that motivates a child to do more chores. Stimulating imagined experiences of that future bicycle fuels energy to rummage through trash for aluminum cans, to babysit little monsters, or even to wash the family car. After we see, taste, touch, smell, and hear a realistic and emotionally compelling future in our imagination, work seems less menial and difficult in relation to the payoff.

Storytelling brings substance to any vision process. When you apply the discipline of interpreting your vision with a story, the process often exposes "plot holes" that may send you back to the drawing board. Building a Vision story is a good way to run thought experiments that can anticipate contrary perceptions or unintended outcomes. Vision stories demand a lot, but they deliver a lot too.

Scenario planning is an underused application of storytelling. Royal Dutch Shell's Scenario Planning team set aside elaborate computer models to predict the future and put the term "scenario planning" on the map after building strategies based on contingency plans that anticipated global events. They had scenarios that predicted the 1973 oil embargo and the fall of the Soviet Union along with a vision for each eventuality.

In scenario planning, strategies are tested in thought experiments against a variety of realistic future stories. This is popularly called a "wind tunnel test" invoking the metaphor of testing aircraft against various weather conditions simulated in a wind tunnel. As with all storytelling, making it tangible produces insights on the plausibility of your vision.

In South Africa during the early 1990s, an incomplete set of government, citizen, and corporate stakeholders engaged in scenario planning at the Mont Fleur Conference Center to craft a common vision for a safe and successful postapartheid South Africa. The country seemed to be leading straight to civil war. Attendees left the event and proceeded to make a series of informal presentations beginning in 1992 that profiled four possible "Mont Fleur scenarios": the "ostrich" (denial and civil war), "lame duck" (weak agreements), "Icarus" (failed pursuit of socialism), or the inspiring "flight of the flamingos" (inclusive democracy and sustainable agreements). Conversations naturally flourished when discussing the "flamingo" option in a way that made the vision of a peaceful transition increasingly plausible, even likely, to a critical mass of citizens.

No scenario could anticipate a man such as Nelson Mandela, but the "flamingo" Vision story surely prepared fertile ground for Dr. Mandela to advise his followers, "If you want to make peace with your enemy, you have to work with your enemy. Then he becomes your partner." Vision stories build a new future first in people's imaginations, because if you can't see it, you can't build it.

Walking around in the virtual reality of a story, you intuitively identify otherwise unpredictable implications, consequences, and correlating factors that are invisible to discussions that stay on a conceptual level. Our purpose here is to build a future story that pulls us in. A "pull" story conjures positive emotions such as desire, hope, belonging, or happiness. Stories based on negative emotions such as *fear* (greed is just another word for fear) fuel stress (also a word for fear) and feed perceptions of danger, scarcity, and us/them thinking. Fear is a physiological and psychological state that narrows vision and limits creativity. The molecules of fear sacrifice peripheral vision in favor of focusing on problems and our three basic human responses: fight, flight, or freeze. Fear can make you stupid. It compartmentalizes every IQ point you have into closed loops of worst-case scenarios.

Hope and love, on the other hand, expand peripheral vision so you can see connections and investigate possibilities only obvious to a relaxed eye. A good Vision story builds resilience and optimism, and at the same time, it validates the difficulties of achieving your vision. "Pie in the sky" visions that ignore real pain, sacrifice, and frustration can burn out your optimists and fail to motivate the realists in your group. You don't want to lose those people or overpromise. That's just borrowing trouble.

Exercise: Develop Your Vision

Before we embark on finding a story, you need to do some groundwork. Begin with your personal vision first. What is your vision? Start by imagining a time 5 to 10 years from now when you have just achieved a set of tangible goals (experiment with a few or conduct a vision trip for each goal one at a time). Let your imagination observe a typical day in tangible detail. You may have to wait, but your imagination will do its job if you are patient. We humans have a huge prefrontal cortex designed specifically for scenario planning in story form. We may as well use it. As the story evolves, your brain will extrapolate from every experience you've ever had to identify plausible opportunities and obstacles as well as fake but useful memories of how you achieved your goals. What was at stake? Who was involved? What happened?

You can illustrate your Vision story like a comic strip or find an analogy that is similar to the achievements, obstacles, and events you imagined. You will find ideas from all four buckets of stories. Ideally, you will find one that blends the *why* and *how* into one. This is a rare gem: a story that not only motivates but also suggests strategies to get there. Read through these four examples of Vision stories to get your ideas flowing, and jot them down as you go along. Give your imagination free rein to explore, anticipate, regroup, and reroute until you have a plausible scenario that feels like success. If it doesn't feel right to you, it won't feel right to anyone else.

A Time You *Shined*

> During the fall of 1992, I was working at J. Walter Thompson in Melbourne, Australia. I had just completed a successful pilot program for the Ford dealer network, set to expand in the next year from a budget of $200,000 to $2 million. The "powers that be" decided to bring in someone with more experience to run "my" program. I didn't take it well. I decided I wasn't cut out for advertising.

Earlier that year in some personal development workshop, I was asked, "If you had all the money in the world, what would you do?" I knew immediately: "I would do something to help groups agree on who they are and why they are here." But my "vision" was so vague that I muddled along without making any real changes. I couldn't envision that future, much less a plan to get there. My subconscious decided to give me a metaphor I could work with.

One night I had a dream that changed everything. I dreamed I was in a big train station with more than 20 platforms. I sat with my mother, drinking coffee, surrounded by our luggage and waiting for our train, which was due in an hour or so. I stood up and announced I was going to walk around a bit. I decided to find our platform and check it out. It was a long walk and down an escalator. As I stood on the platform, our train arrived, an hour early, and the loudspeaker said it was leaving in three minutes. I didn't have my luggage. I didn't have a ticket. My mother didn't know where I was, but I got on anyway.

If I took the time to get everything I needed, I would miss the train. I distinctly remember thinking, "I'll just have to make it up as I go," and I began practicing my explanation for the first problem I'd encounter: no ticket to show the guy who checks tickets.

When I woke up that next morning, I knew I would quit my job, move back to the United States, find a graduate program or a mentor, and invent a new career. Some people thought I was having a meltdown, my mother in particular. Common sense says you need to have a job before you quit one, at the very least a general idea of a job description. I had neither. On April 23, 1993, I flew home to Louisiana, drove across country that June, and by August I had found both a graduate program and a mentor. By 1997, I had a graduate degree, two years' experience with my mentor, and a contract for my first book. When the book came out, I started my own business. My Vision story told me to just get on the train without a ticket or luggage and figure out the details as they arose.

A Vision story carved in stone is not as good as one that is loose enough to adapt and change along the way.

A Time You *Blew It*

One of my first bosses had to see every letter I wrote and critiqued my presentation before I was allowed to send a letter or deliver the presentation to our client. Letters came back from her dense with red pen marks, deleted sentences, and scribbled rewrites. Presentations were rearranged and reworded to Linda's satisfaction. I didn't fight her. I had lost all my confidence the year before in a rather brutal public-speaking course, where the instructor stopped us in the middle of an extemporaneous speech for other participants to vote you on or off the stage. I was devastated. *Survivor* may make good TV, but it's not a nurturing format for developing good communication skills.

These highly edited presentations were boring, awkward, and painful for me and everyone else. I am not a very good marionette. One day, I was asked to present a status report in Linda's absence. She was off getting her boobs done. I had no taskmaster to please, so I just did it my way. I delivered a 15-minute presentation that for once wasn't designed to avoid her red pen but was instead designed to please the client. And boy, did it please the client. I was embarrassed by praise that seemed to ask, "What was your problem before?" The client congratulated my boss's boss because the only explanation that made sense to them was that my newly coherent and smooth delivery must have been a result of his mentoring. He just smiled and gave me a wink.

From that day forward, I vowed to never deliver someone else's words or someone else's message. I decided I would be myself, speak in my style with my own words, and pay the price if I blew it. I knew that if I couldn't make the message mine, then I should rethink the message.

A Mentor

If you have ever gotten into trouble for telling the truth, then we have something in common. I've been blabbing uncomfortable truths or naming elephants that might have sat happily unnamed ever since I was five years old. Rather than an extra dose of courage, I suspect my behavior is better described as a certain lack of discretion. But since that's who I am, I need skills to handle what happens next. I embraced the archetype of heretic and looked for a successful heretic story that would teach me how to tell the truth and not get burned at the stake. I found a mentor in the man Galileo. He is one of my favorite truth tellers for lots of reasons, but most of all because he stuck by his truth without burning at the stake. One of his contemporaries, Bruno, said the exact same things Galileo said, and he was burned at the stake. Galileo's final punishment was house arrest at an age when traveling was difficult anyway.

People can tell me all day long that I "have to pick my battles," but I can't seem to translate that advice into a tangible strategy. Galileo's story is much more helpful. He had powerful friends and a diplomatic relationship with "the truth." To survive the Inquisition, Galileo actually signed a confession admitting that he was wrong and asserting that the sun orbited the earth. After that, he continued to write and speak, and he stayed under the radar until finally confined to his own house in Florence in his seventies.

I regularly ask myself, "W.W.G.D.?" *What would Galileo do?* His biography is a Vision story to me. Legend has it that Galileo received a letter from a friend begging him to intervene and save Bruno from burning, but he declined. Maybe he stayed silent because he didn't have enough clout or maybe he chose to save himself instead. It reminds me of the serenity prayer phrase, "the wisdom to know the difference." Galileo had a passion for the truth, but he did not choose to become a martyr. When the pope forced Galileo to sign that confession, Galileo folded like a cheap tent.

But Galileo's best strategy was to write a story in which three characters argue the virtues and validity of both sides of the argument. He published his story

in a book titled *The Dialogue of Two World Systems* just
four years before he died. It is still in print. Galileo let
his characters say what he could not and ask questions
that exposed the truth he was forbidden from discussing. Galileo was a crafty old coot. He was dedicated to
the truth, flexible enough to moderate his approach, and
willing to silence his ego when danger threatened—
lessons I try to remember.

Every human drama is to some extent a repeat of
one that went before. If you look closely, you will find an
individual you admire who has already overcome obstacles and pursued goals remarkably similar to your own.

A Book, Movie, or Current Event

There are plenty of movies that offer great Vision stories. *Miracle* (2004), about the 1980 US ice-hockey team,
teaches about cohesion. *Seabiscuit* (2003) represents the
galvanizing spirit of the underdog. *The Greatest Game Ever
Played* (2005) straightens my spine as it reminds me that I
decide who I am and where I belong. But all these movies
are about competition and sports, where there are winners
and losers.

I enjoy contests, but my overarching vision for my
life is not a competition. More than a decade ago, I
decided to live my life as an artist. I think businesses
and organizations need art as much as any other part
of society. I'm also from the South. So it might be no
surprise that I turn to Johnny Cash.

Johnny Cash was a prolific artist. During his recording career starting in 1955, he is said to have written well

over 1,000 songs. He released more than 153 singles and 96 albums. After 1968, when Johnny married June Carter and got his addictions under control, it seems that most fights with his "handlers" were over issues of authenticity. He wrote in his autobiography, *Cash*, that he got tired of his record company, CBS, advising him with demographics of the "new country fan," the "new market profile," and all the other trends derived with statistics.[4] By 1974, he felt "mentally divorced" from CBS. So Cash gave CBS a record called "Chicken in Black," which was "intentionally atrocious." He even forced CBS to pay for a video shot in New York City where he dressed up like a chicken. The next year, 1986, CBS declined to renew his contract. Big surprise. Johnny Cash had discovered civil disobedience.

I love this story because it supports my natural inclination to reject numbers that don't create a meaningful connection I can feel in my bones. If it doesn't feel right, I don't do it. Johnny Cash's long career proves that standing his ground paid off. At age 61, he had a comeback that reached deep into the very demographics CBS would've killed for. Producer Rick Rubin, "in clothes that would've done a wino proud," convinced Cash that he would produce whatever music Cash wanted to record. Rubin, producer of the Red Hot Chili Peppers and Beastie Boys, told him he wasn't very familiar with the music Cash loved, but he wanted to hear all of it. Cash questioned Rubin's assumption that his music could appeal to a younger audience. He thought it unlikely. Rubin answered

---

4. Johnny Cash, *Cash: The Autobiography* (New York: HarperOne, 2003).

that "they only need to see the fire and passion you bring to your music . . . just be totally honest." That honesty produced four Grammy-winning albums.

Authenticity, the good and the bad, is synonymous with the Cash legend. Johnny Cash's life is a testament to never giving up on your art and to never selling out. When I wear my Johnny Cash t-shirt, strangers give me the thumbs-up sign in the grocery store. It's validating.

One final note: In my humble opinion, fiction is a dangerous place to go hunting for Vision stories because even great fiction is an invented world that may have been idealized and was certainly manipulated to grab and keep attention. The benefit of true stories is that they actually happened (at least once), so it seems more likely that you could make them happen again.

CHAPTER 9

Value-in-Action Stories

JUST ABOUT EVERY story you tell about a disaster with a cable company, plumber, electrician, or other contractor could be considered a Value-in-Action story. The same goes for air travel stories. These tend to be disaster stories that profile selfish or apathetic values, and we tell them so often that we have a bad habit of playing the "Can you top this?" game.

Consider that Derrick the plumber came to my house on a Saturday morning an hour after I called. He had his young son in tow, and they were on their way to a soccer game. Even so, Derrick took the time to fix a leak in my guest bathroom because my mom was coming to visit on Sunday. He went above and beyond the call of duty. He demonstrated values of respect, love of family, punctuality, generosity, and competence.

Then there was Ted, who, after two no-shows, arrived late, did a lousy job installing a new back door, and sent an invoice for twice his original quote. His is a story of procrastination, disrespect, and dishonesty.

The Ted story sits at the tip of my tongue, while the Derrick story doesn't have the same resonance. Everything went right. Derrick met and exceeded my expectations. Yet his story ignites fewer strong emotions.

Common sense tells me that sharing the Derrick story is more likely to leave me feeling inspired to go above and beyond myself, because in telling it, I reinforce my feeling that the world is full of generous people. It reflects my own good values.

On the other hand, the second story leaves me feeling cynical. I remember how people can be selfish and unreliable. The story doesn't leave me feeling eager to reach out and help others. Even so, that Ted story wants to jump in and compete for the "worst contractor ever" award whenever a conversation turns to contractor stories.

That's partly because telling a disaster story helps us process emotions and move past bad experiences. But it is healthier to move past refueling negative emotions by looping through the same story over and over and to move on or reframe disaster stories with a positive message. Value-in-Action stories build either inspiration, creativity and innovation, or frustration and apathy. I'll discuss how to do so in a bit, but first, let's look at the many ways that values can translate to stories that fit into our everyday lives.

Metaphors as Mini Value Stories

The stories and metaphors we use in everyday communication lay the foundation for how we think about the world—our value system. Metaphors are ministories that help us frame complexity into a familiar package. We use the war metaphor a lot: the war on AIDS, for instance. When we channel our desire to find a cure and prevent the spread of AIDS through the metaphor of war, it feels more urgent and, for some people, more "winnable." Many people like the metaphor of war because it makes them feel stronger and inspired to fight. It triggers their fight-or-flight responses and stimulates adrenaline and cortisol that push people into action. War feels active, while "healing a disease" is gentler and more complex (and in some cases may produce better insights).

Metaphors frame and simplify, but at the same time, they can compartmentalize and oversimplify. We are often suckered into metaphors that stir our emotions and direct our resources in ways we might not choose if we were paying closer attention. For instance, it is commonly accepted that factories, products, or information systems function best as "lean, mean, fighting machines." This metaphor helps you "trim the fat" (metaphor) and "get rid of deadwood" (metaphor). But consider how these metaphors translate when applied to people. Yes, people can be "lean, mean, fighting machines" too. Perhaps you've dealt with a few of those machine-like people. You might have felt like a machine yourself. You are left with a dead feeling, because the "lean, mean, fighting machine" metaphor can dull our humanity and disconnect us from the empathy one flawed human has for another—it kills the values that preserve human and humane systems.

When a company uses the metaphor "flawless execution" to describe its accounting services, that's good. That is exactly what I want when someone files my taxes: flawless execution. But that company also needs complementary metaphors to accommodate the people side—the complex individuals who exist outside popular conceptions of perfection. The "customer is always right" is a popular metaphor, but this notion only works when it is tempered with values such as trust, tolerance, reciprocity, and forgiveness that accommodate the ambiguities of real life. The fact is, the customer is not always right.

One evening—hassled, tired, and angry that my hotel key didn't work—I marched downstairs to the front desk and showed the card key to the desk clerk saying, "This key doesn't work." I probably even let out an exasperated sigh.

The desk clerk grinned ear to ear with a twinkle in his eye and said, "That might be because this key isn't for our hotel."

I looked and sure enough the key I was holding was for the hotel I'd just left. I was wrong and I had been rude, but his mood lifted mine and I grinned back.

"Well, then, that would be the reason it doesn't work. Wouldn't it?"

We shared a joke on me.

Mr. "Flawless Execution" could have embarrassed me for being stupid *and* rude. Instead, this man chose to forgive, have some fun, and help me save face in spite of my being quite flawed. Together, we created a "the customer is not always right" story.

It's Not Bragging

Integrity, by definition, is doing the right thing when no one would have ever known if you cheated, acted selfishly, or fudged a number. That is, integrity-in-action usually occurs without any witnesses. If you don't tell your story, no one will ever know that you did the right thing. It's not bragging. Besides, integrity means different things to different people.

For my father, a retired federal employee and a lieutenant colonel in the Army Reserve, integrity meant that if his boss told him to do something, he did it. To me, integrity means if my client asks me to do something that feels wrong, I have to say no. I wouldn't promote stories of trust for a company that exploits people, despite the reward it might bring me.

Values are never clear-cut. That's why Value-in-Action stories are vital if you genuinely want to build collective values powerful enough to guide behavior. In a campaign for more civility between employees, Jim Falucci of Veterans Affairs in New York shared a story with his staff about successfully shifting values toward smoking in VA hospitals. Jim talks about a day when people didn't look twice at smokers in the hospital. No one explicitly said smoking was OK. It was implicitly OK. Change began when people weren't supposed to smoke in the elevators. Jim described his frustration when he was the only person willing to correct a stranger getting on an elevator with a lit cigarette. "Now," he says, "woe to anyone who dares light up inside the building, much less the elevator."

His story draws attention to the correlation between speaking up and changing behavior. He compared incivility with smoking. No one seemed willing to speak out against incivility, so it was tolerated in some pockets of the hospital system. Incivility seemed to be implicitly OK.

It takes courage to be one of the first in your organization to stop tolerating a behavior such as smoking or incivility. Values often cost you something in the short term. I recall a warm conversation that chilled when I asked a relative to refrain from using racist language. It cost me in the short term but has increased awareness in my family over the long term. Values don't pay off without continuous investment by real people who face real consequences for holding fast to values, and that's why Value-in-Action stories are so important.

An organization that professes to value respect should be teeming with stories about showing respect when it wasn't easy. If you can't find stories about respect, it doesn't necessarily mean you aren't a good story gatherer. It may mean, instead, that other values are currently more important than respect. I worked with a global company concerned with "hygiene issues"—their metaphor for low trust levels in their market. At the time, this company was peerless when it came to identifying and exploiting market and product opportunities. They truly were one of the best companies in the world in terms of making the right decisions and exploiting opportunities and partnerships to make money and grow their market share.

That year, they had so many new products to introduce they called it the "season of swagger." I was asked to help find a story highlighting their trustworthiness. Instead, I called attention to current stories being told by suppliers, customers, and partners. It seems that the values of speed, excellence, and growth meant they regularly abandoned or ignored partners by labeling them as slow or subpar. Exploiting every opportunity to chase growth justified behaviors that looked mighty untrustworthy to these partners and clients—in other words, they were trading rapid growth for trustworthiness.

Taking Cultural Values into Account

Each culture prizes different values. Mix two cultures and you better start sharing Value-in-Action stories. Otherwise you will end up with assumptions that "they aren't trustworthy" or "they don't have integrity," when in truth, they simply have a different definition of those values.

Mixing cultures produces both creativity and misunderstanding. But if you understand each group's cultural values, these groups tackle very predictable conflicts. You can reduce distrust and engender creativity by investing time for sharing Value-in-Action stories that give everyone an opportunity to express their personal values in a way that makes sense and does not feel judgmental to those with a radically different background. Ask an American whether, when witnessing a hit-and-run accident, he or she would turn the driver in, and he or she won't think twice about an emphatic "Yes!" Anyone would, right? Not in some cultures. A Venezuelan witnessing a hit-and-run accident might pretend he or she didn't see a thing, particularly if that person was his or her boss. He or she has a family to feed.

Many heated disagreements can be resolved when people meet a conflict after they have shared Value-in-Action stories that address the values they feel are in question. It is an unfortunate consequence of American ethnocentricity that we tend to treat our national values as common sense or rational thinking. Not everyone believes that the early bird should get the worm or that you have to blow your own horn. Values emerged to simulate clarity in ambiguous circumstances.

Like many values, for instance, trust is not strictly rational. Trust means I can fall and you won't leave me. Trust means that if I sacrifice for your good, you will return the favor in the future. Trust rates good intentions over current results and allows for second chances. Objective reasoning alone is too constraining to inspire or cultivate loyalty from complex humans. Even a rational and reasonable decision to kill a product line can leave a product manager with hard feelings about how the decision went down or was communicated.

International experience is a good way to decrease blind trust in your own definition of rational thinking. When your experience comes from only one culture, certain conclusions seem obvious. You run the risk of missing the arbitrary nature of cultural definitions of values such as integrity, trust, and success. An American who thinks it is obvious that any good compensation system rewards individual efforts can easily get on the wrong side of a Japanese manager who believes just as emphatically that any good compensation system ensures no individuals seem more important than the group as a whole.

Exercise: Identify Your Values

It is not only good business sense but also critical to your sense of happiness to know your values and feel that you live up to your own standards. Before you look for stories, take some time to think and write down the four most important values that guide your behavior. These change over time, and at any point in your life, some will have higher priority than others. (If you don't mind paying a fee, there is an online survey at http://www.valuesperspectivesbook.com that will give you a report on your current top values.) Think about a time when you had to decide between several unacceptable options. If your choice left you feeling like you did the right thing, you probably based your decision on a value. If it left you feeling you did the wrong thing, you neglected a value that was part of your internal guidance system.

A Time You *Shined*

For a long time, I ran a facilitator training course based on my second book, *A Safe Place for Dangerous Truths*. It is based on a formal approach that temporarily intensifies a large group's dialogue so individuals feel safe to reveal hidden agendas and "dangerous truths." This type of dialogue is not for the weak-hearted. The facilitator course is limited to 10 participants because participants need to sort through baggage about how people "should" behave in groups and what facilitation "should" be, and it's a very personal process.

The course was in January, and by November, I had five people enrolled. I was probably not going to fill the class, but I always run it anyway. The phone rang, and the representative of a large organization asked me how many places I had left. I told him I had five places left.

He said, "We'll take all five."

Now, that might seem like good news, but I was thrust into a moral quandary. Each of the five already enrolled participants was self-employed or paying their own way. Each of them worked in different types of industries. If you have ever attended a course where 50 percent of the participants are from the same organization, you know that group discussions are dominated by examples from the organization that makes up the majority of the class. I felt it would be unfair to the original five people who had signed up. Plus, each of them paid out of pocket, and the five prospective participants would be attending on their company's dime.

In all good conscience, I had to say, "I'm afraid I can't take five people from the same organization. It wouldn't be fair to the rest of the group. I can take two now, and we can figure out something in between now and next year or just let them take the course next year."

There was a long pause on the other end of the line. "Are you telling me no? You are refusing enrollment?"

I tried to explain my reasoning, but he would have none of it. "Then we won't be sending anyone."

I said, "I'm sorry you feel that way." I was sorry to lose the opportunity, but I still feel like I did the right thing.

You learn your values over time by having those values tested. A core value manifests itself when you chose that value over an easier, cheaper, or faster alternative that feels wrong in some way. The choices you make to go with values you know are the right ones, and the circumstances surrounding those choices, are shining examples that will make excellent Value-in-Action stories.

There have been many occasions when your values were tested. All you have to do is choose one of those instances and tell about a time when it would have been easier to do anything but follow your values. Respect, reliability, precision, trustworthiness, compassion, or winning: in every case, you chose the more difficult path your core values demanded of you. Tell about all the circumstances, and be honest about whether you deliberated over your decision. It makes the story more real to know that you almost didn't do the "right thing."

A Time You *Blew It*

Frankly, I did not expect teaching storytelling at a Navy base would be so enlightening. I was wrong. Our military attracts some of the finest men and women in our country and gives many who would not otherwise begin life with fine qualities the opportunity to develop them. This is a story within a story, but I'm including both because sometimes stories aren't the same when they're cut in two. And in this case, it adds a mentor story as a bonus.

Sixty men and women sat in the training room. The course was open enrollment and, departing from normal military protocol, the participants ranged from very high to low rank, sitting side by side. Both great and small sat together in those chair-desks I remember from high school. Storytelling is a great equalizer.

When we broke for lunch, the group swiftly headed to the galley—except one guy. I hadn't noticed him before. He was small, compact, redheaded, and freckled, one of those people who could be 14 or 40; it was impossible to tell. We were the last two in the otherwise empty room. I couldn't figure out what he was waiting for. I was waiting for the training manager, Bettye Bruemuller, to come get me. She and I were going off base for lunch.

She glanced at him as we walked out and said, "End of the month, I just hate that." I looked bewildered and she went on: "He's broke—no money for lunch until payday at the end of the week. I see it all the time."

I glanced back. He was looking out the window.

We got into Bettye's big red Cadillac (she has style) and headed off to get some greens and cornbread. On our way back, she gave no explanation as she pulled into the Chick-fil-A drive-thru. She continued chatting in between ordering a sandwich and drink. I assumed someone had asked her to pick something up.

When we returned, she walked me back to the training room and came inside to set the sandwich and drink on a side table, announcing to the room in general, "Some idiot screwed up our order and gave us an extra sandwich. I didn't want it to go to waste. I figured one of you boys might want it." As I said, Bettye has style. I left for a minute, and when I came back, "Red" was slurping down the end of his drink and the bag was wadded up on his desktop.

I smiled, called the class to order, and asked who would be willing to share a story next. His hand went up like a shot. I invited him to come to the front, and he told this story.

"I joined the Navy because this girl I liked joined. Of course, I never saw her again." He paused for the laughter. "But it didn't matter because for the next 14 years, I was either drunk or stoned most of the time. Two years ago, I self-referred myself into a treatment program. It was my own decision. I haven't had any drugs or alcohol for two years."

"When I sobered up, I learned something really important: I *hate* the Navy!" He had to wait a long time for the laughter to die down. "As a matter of fact, I hate authority in general. But I only have a few more years until I can retire with full benefits. When I retire, I'm getting as far away from this life as humanly possible.

> But until that day, as long as I'm here, I want every one
> of you to know you can count on me. I will go where I'm
> told, when I'm told, and do what I'm told."
>
> The entire room broke into spontaneous applause. A
> few of the guys slapped him on the back as he returned
> to his chair. Owning up to what might otherwise feel
> shameful is difficult, but it is a ticket to emotional free-
> dom. When you tell a story like this, people deeply
> appreciate the depth of humility required to admit that
> you failed your own value system once upon a time.

I recommend you look for a story from a chapter in your
life that is already closed. You need to be long past feeling
shamed by this event. Don't tell it until you have forgiven
yourself and have come out the other side. They say tragedy
plus time is comedy. Wait until you can laugh about it a little
before you tell this kind of Value-in-Action story.

Look for stories from the times when you should've done
the right thing but, for whatever reason, you didn't. There is
not a human being alive who doesn't carry these stories. The
power of the story lies dormant until you tell it. You will be
amazed at how many people will come up to thank you for
telling a story about a time when you failed your own standards. It's obvious you aren't condoning failure. What you are
doing is demonstrating humility. We all stumble.

A Mentor

Everyone should have a Value-in-Action story that illustrates what integrity means to them. Bettye in the previous
story mentored me to see that integrity can mean seeking out

opportunities to demonstrate your values: in her case, generosity and kindness. Once, teaching a roomful of 2,000 retail-electronics sales staff, I asked them to share a story of integrity with a partner. I was pretty sure they'd come up with stories better suited to their culture than I could. They did. I love this particular story because it is such a "guy" story.

> I come to a lot of these conferences. Most of them, like this one in Las Vegas, are surrounded by casinos. I enjoy gambling, but I don't enjoy losing. So my buddy Jack and I made a deal where we spread the risk. Whenever we go to a casino together, we split our winnings 50/50. It makes it more fun, and we have twice the chance to leave a winner.
>
> So last night, we were playing blackjack and a little roulette, and I was losing. I was tired anyway, so I decided to go to bed early, if you call 1 a.m. early. Anyway, this morning I'm sitting at breakfast, and Jack walks up like a Cheshire cat and slams down $1,500 in cash right next to my coffee cup.
>
> I asked him, "What the hell is this?"
>
> He says, "We won last night! Three thousand smackeroos, and this is your share!"
>
> I told him, "Man, this is your money, not mine. I wimped out on you last night."
>
> He just screwed up his face like I was nuts and says, "A deal is a deal," and walks off.
>
> Now, that's what I call integrity. He didn't have to share that money with me. I'm not sure that I would've. But I can guarantee that I will in the future. A deal is a deal.

What mentor taught you how to do the right thing? Who in your industry, culture, or organization epitomizes the best of the best? If you seek to influence outside your own group, you might seek a mentor figure from the culture, history, or ethnicity of your listeners. Don't assume that your mentor will be someone else's mentor when it comes to values. The extra research pays off.

When speaking to your own family, organization, or cultural group, all you have to do is find stories of people most admired by this group, and you will find Value-in-Action stories. Look to those you admire personally to find examples of your own values in action. It is fun to arbitrarily choose one of your favorite stories about someone you admire and then decode it for the value(s) illustrated in that story.

A Book, Movie, or Current Event

Sara Lawrence-Lightfoot's marvelous book *Respect* is basically a book of Respect-in-Action stories.[5] Among those wonderful stories, she tells one about Jennifer Dohrn, who was a nurse-midwife in a clinic in the South Bronx. To me, the most striking detail of Jennifer's story was that Jennifer dressed up for the birth of every baby. When the time was near, she put on her best jewelry, gorgeous clothes, and full makeup, so that "when the baby arrives, his or her first view of life outside of the womb will be lovely."

When I first started speaking, I got some negative comments on evaluation forms about my clothing. They said I was

---

5.   Sara Lawrence-Lightfoot, *Respect: An Exploration* (Reading, Mass.: Perseus, 2000).

too casual, even "unprofessional." I wasn't dressing like a hussy but more like a frump. This was before the cable show *What Not to Wear*, or I might have ended up on it. I was under the impression that what I said was more important than how I looked.

The story I borrowed from the book about Jennifer Dohrn helped me see that my clothing can be viewed as a statement of my respect for others. Over the years, I've learned that respect is communicated in a thousand subtle details beyond my extremely reasoned, rational way of thinking. This story in particular communicates how paying attention to symbolic details can communicate to others in a tangible way.

> How would a baby know whether Jennifer had applied lipstick or not? She pointed out that the baby's mother would know. The baby's father and siblings would notice. Their behavior might begin to match hers. She's setting an example with lipstick that might result in more gentle handling, more time cooing, or even an internal commitment to improve the family's standard of living.
>
> Just as important, Jennifer knows. She described dressing up for those babies in a way that clearly demonstrated the respect she has for all human life, rich or poor. Like Jennifer, I now pay attention to my clothing and makeup so that anyone can tell at a glance that I'm honored to be hired to train or speak to a group and that I'm grateful for the opportunity to learn their stories.

Like Vision stories, I think it is important to stay wary of idealized Value-in-Action stories. If a story lacks believability in a movie or in your reading, you probably can't make it seem believable in a Value-in-Action story.

Sometimes a brief summary of the plot can illustrate a value. Don't turn your nose up at TV shows. More people might connect to a Value-in-Action story from *The Simpsons* than to a recap of a Dostoyevsky novel.

CHAPTER 10

I-Know-What-You-Are-Thinking Stories

WHEN A UNION representative meets with a manager to resolve a grievance, both enter the room with preconceptions. They may believe they are entering with open minds, but our minds stand guard over our best interests, whether we ask them to or not. Secret suspicions usually lurk beneath hearty handshakes and wide smiles. Ms. Manager might secretly think the union guy is full of himself, high on temporary power, or a troublemaker milking a conflict for its drama opportunities. Mr. Union may secretly suspect that Ms. Manager is a ball-busting bitch on wheels who has it in for the gal he is representing because of some "woman thing." Either one of them could break the ice and score points by telling a good I-Know-What-You-Are-Thinking story.

Mr. Union might tell "what my dad taught me about abusing power," or Ms. Manager could relate a story about her first job "when I acted like a bitch and regretted it." Either story could dramatically change the atmosphere. I-Know-What-You-Are-Thinking stories overcome unspoken objections without coming off as oppositional and may actually validate the other person.

The Power of Validation

Humans hunger for validation. It doesn't cost you a thing, and sometimes you get tangible concessions in return. Meanwhile, failing to validate another's point of view can cost you twice the time, money, or effort you might otherwise spend influencing a person. Anyone who has seen couples confront one another on reality TV has surely learned that invalidation escalates conflict. Even if you think your partner's feelings are ridiculous and not at all what you "meant" her to feel, explaining one more time how she "should" feel makes things worse. When he says to her, "You are being ridiculous," and she says to him, "You are an insensitive clod," both are invalidating the other.

Even if the statements are technically accurate (and often they are), they make things worse. Miraculously, if he would say, "I can see how my little joke about your painting might have felt like a criticism," and she would say, "It makes sense that you would point out that I painted the males with proportions that are anatomically unlikely," they could relax. They could feel free to be less defensive and more open.

Many arguments are fueled less by the "need to be right" and more by the chronically unmet need to be heard and respected. That's where I-Know-What-You-Are-Thinking stories come into play. They overcome objections and allow you to tip your hat and show your audience respect.

A case in point is a surgeon I met who felt frustrated by failed attempts to convince his staff to stop taking his outbursts and snippy retorts personally. The situation was not unusual: surgeons require big egos to slice into someone's flesh, but a big ego can translate into a lack of respect for others, and as a result, many surgeons find that their support staff are less supportive than they expect. What this surgeon neglected to do was validate the fact that his staff were as personally committed to patient safety as he was. He's adapted the practice of telling an I-Know-What-You-Are-Thinking story that apologizes in advance for when he slips into the state of focus where "nothing and no one else matters." He explains that he understands how his concentration might appear dismissive but that he values the role of others as much as he does his own. His story validates his support staff as people and fine colleagues well enough that they tolerate the side effects of his hyperfocus.

Telepathic Powers

Telling a good I-Know-What-You-Are-Thinking story can make your listeners think that you have read their minds and know their secret thoughts. This level of validation and insight into your audience's point of view can earn you big points.

Try to identify the hidden suspicions held by your intended audience. It doesn't take a genius to do so. When you welcome objections into the light of day, they often shrivel and disappear in the sunlight of open examination.

In the military, hierarchical status and clearance usually correlate so closely that the two are interpreted interchangeably. If you have high clearance, you must be important. If you are important, you have high security clearance. I don't have a high security clearance. Therefore I can anticipate that many of my military clients might naturally wonder how smart or important I could possibly be. So I bring the issue into the open and reframe it.

I was working with Air Force Intelligence, and the "big guy" insisted I join his group for dinner.

He told me, "We need to get you security clearance."

I told him, "No way."

He pulled his chin down and looked at me over his glasses as if I either was dealing drugs or had a body hidden somewhere. I explained, "You don't want to give me security clearance because I can't be trusted."

OK, I was playing with him a little here, but it was too tempting to resist. Before he could launch into me, I continued, "To prepare for this course, I made a big yellow file that I labeled 'Air Force Intelligence.' Last week I had a pedicure, and I took this big yellow file to read at the salon. I finished my pedicure, walked out, and left the big yellow file in the salon—sitting right on top of the other reading material. I do that sort of thing all the time. I am absentminded."

I then explained that I did not inherit the genetic code for keeping secrets and that I sometimes think that I wrote the book *A Safe Place for Dangerous Truths* simply to decrease the number of secrets I'm expected to keep. However, I told him, I strongly believe it is one of the main reasons I'm good at what I do. I make tools and design methods that decrease the amount of unnecessary secrecy clogging the lines of communication. "My value to you is much higher without security clearance," I summed up.

My story highlighted the hidden association between "important" and "security clearance" and destabilized the relationship long enough for me to make a case that the two aren't always interchangeable. If I didn't do this up front, I might have lost my opportunity.

Framing

When setting up an I-Know-What-You-Are-Thinking story, remember that it is much easier to exert influence if you can control the sequence of information that best supports your point of view. For instance, the "after" pictures that advertise a diet wouldn't sell many diet plans without the "before" pictures. I highly recommend *Influence: Science and Practice* by Robert Cialdini.[6] One of my favorite examples from his book cites a letter from a college freshman to her parents. In the beginning of her letter, she tells her parents that her skull fracture is healing, the fire wasn't so bad after the janitor offered to let her stay with him, and oh, by the way, they are expecting a baby together. Her last paragraph reveals that there was no skull fracture, no fire, no janitor, and no pregnancy, *but* she did get a "D" in chemistry and just wanted to put the bad grade into the proper perspective.

Perspective can make a $100 donation seem huge (feed a family for a year) and tiny (one month of mocha lattes)

---

6. Robert Cialdini, *Influence: Science and Practice* (Boston: Allyn and Bacon, 2001).

in the same letter. Fundraisers improve perceptions of target donation amounts by listing that amount as a second option dwarfed by a huge amount in the first option. Saying "no" to a first request leaves a donor with a lingering sense of obligation that increases the likelihood of a "yes" to the second request. Children learn this trick early. The question "Mommy, can Billy and I ride our bikes to the gun show?" gets a quick "no" that makes the next question, "Then can Billy come over to play?" seem like a bargain.

Exercise: Pay Attention to What Others Are Thinking

Zero in on the positive intent behind a potential objection. Particularly, if you fear a hostile audience, dig down and find the positive intent that drives their objections and honor their intent with a story that broadens their current interpretation of what is objectionable. Be careful to never belittle another person's caution; rather, the point is to validate it and move on.

A Time You *Shined*

As a facilitator, I am often lumped in with a collection of bad experiences a group may have had with "facilitator types." We've all had bad experiences. Even smart, optimistic groups are wary of some stranger who proposes to lead (control) their process and agenda for two days. Sometimes I start by telling this story.

> My favorite introduction by a client to a group hap-
> pened in Aspen. A group of very smart, very successful

executives gathered to work and play for a weekend. The woman who introduced me said, "This is Annette. I promise you, she doesn't use chimes."

They applauded. I knew there was a good story behind her choice of words. They told about their last retreat, where they had a "woo-woo" facilitator in long, flowing clothes who used chimes to indicate the end of breaks. The group may have been slow to come back after breaks, and I imagined the chime lady getting a little passive-aggressive with her chimes. During the next break, someone kidnapped her chimes and left a ransom note. The best part of the retreat for them was the series of ransom notes and the increasingly less "woo-woo" reactions of the chime lady.

So I promised no chimes, no "woo-woo" stuff, no holding hands, no singing "Kumbaya." And I assured them that any discussion about feelings would have a business application.

A Time You *Blew It*

Teaching leadership is a perfect time to implement I-Know-What-You-Are-Thinking stories. One of my recent experiences was with a group of women in Europe who might have considered my American mannerisms to be rather brusque. I told them a story.

> When I was in elementary school, I liked to be left in charge of anything because it made me feel special. I was naturally bossy. In sixth grade, I was given a little sheriff's badge and was told to watch the first graders

during recess on rainy days so the first-grade teacher could get a break. To entertain them (or me), I taught them how to march in formation with band music. I'm not making this up. I rewarded those who participated with peppermint candies. I was a little monster. Nice kids slipped the nonparticipating kids candies, and my reward system was immediately diffused with lack of compliance. I learned you can't mandate cooperation.

Years later, as an adult, I was able to tell this story and acknowledge their concerns about my brusqueness and at the same time reassure them that I don't endorse command-and-control leadership. I let them know that I wanted them to call me out if they saw me going too fast or making faulty assumptions.

A Mentor

Teaching the staff of the United States Agency for International Development (USAID) to tell stories was one of my favorite jobs ever. The men and women of this organization could single-handedly earn back any of the love and appreciation the United States has lost, if only the world could hear their stories.

These are some of the smartest, most dedicated people I've ever had the privilege to know. Most speak several languages, have lived in many cultures, and hold doctorates in an array of complicated subjects. However, the story I want to tell you here is a mixed bag I use specifically with USAID people because they can be very hard on themselves. There are times when smart, high achievers can only become better leaders after they learn to forgive themselves for their mistakes.

One of the most articulate and beautiful women I've met in a long time was in a USAID group. She seemed to have inherited the carriage and dignity of the African queens she was surely descended from. Growing up in a ghetto of Detroit did not bend her. After getting advanced degrees and joining the Foreign Service, she spent much of her time in Africa. Her last post had been in Nigeria, where this story occurred.

She started her story this way:

I sent my eight-year-old daughter to a local public school in Nigeria. When I was asked to serve on the school board, I happily accepted. However, the board wanted me to chair. I declined, saying that the chair should be a Nigerian rather than a foreigner. I actively lobbied for a particular Nigerian woman who had a Ph.D. in education and who was very visible in the community. Sure, I heard a few warnings about this woman's character, but I felt the issue of citizenship was more important.

(She then paused for a really long time and foreshadowed the rest of the story by saying, "She really did seem qualified.")

Once we started having meetings, I saw the problem. This woman was arrogant, opinionated, rude, and controlling. She had no idea how to run a meeting. They went too long, and even after they were over, every board member would call me up that night to complain and ask me to do something. It was taking over my life, so I finally agreed. I told them I'd speak to her at the next meeting as long as they would back me up.

At that next meeting, this woman started doing what she always did. She cut people off. She railroaded her agenda items. So I asked if I could make a comment on the process. She turned to me, and to this day I have no idea what happened. All I know is that I lost it. I lit into that woman like Hell's fury. I called her every name except child of God. I have no idea how long it lasted, but when my eyes started to refocus, I suddenly saw myself surrounded by wide eyes and dropped jaws.

I said, "I think I should leave now," and got myself the hell out of there.

I got home, sat down, and thought, "What have I done?" I was horrified. Within the hour, I realized what I had to do. I started at the top of the list and called each and every member and apologized. The next day, I went in person and apologized to her. She was less than gracious, but I kept my dignity.

When I tell this story, I'm talking about myself, too. I get passionate about issues, and sometimes I can be short with people. I have a temper, and if I could have had it surgically removed, I would have. But it seems to be here to stay, so I try to apologize in advance. I can't guarantee that I won't "lose it" at some point as a long-term member of a working group. But I can guarantee that I will correct myself quickly and apologize.

You may find an analogy of your circumstances either in your own past, in a historical event, or preferably in the history of your target audience. Do some research to see if you can find whether the current problem isn't a repeat of a pattern of problems for this particular culture or work group.

A Book, Movie, or Current Event

Anyone who has served on a neighborhood committee has experienced the full range of insanity that simple issues can invoke in otherwise sane people. In my old neighborhood, the insanity erupted over a motion to redistrict our 1920s enclave as a historical district. The neighborhood was modest and diverse. Many professors from the local university lived there, and some front yards contained bizarre sculptures. Two families thought Christmas lights presented a year-round opportunity to express themselves, and several neighbors had sustainable ecosystems instead of grass in their front yards. We may not have liked the paint color of our neighbors' home, but we would have died defending their right to paint it whatever color they wanted to.

After years of peaceful diversity, a young lawyer moved in and was quickly elected president of our local neighborhood association. He did everything in his power to push a redistricting effort I referred to as the "hysterical district" era. The ensuing conflict pitted neighbor against neighbor. One guy painted his house purple and pink in protest. Long meetings, angry letters, and plots to undermine the "other side" replaced potluck, pumpkin-carving parties. I was asked to come before the board for a violation, so I began with an I-Know-What-You-Are-Thinking story.

We are North Carolinians, so I suspect all of us here have seen at least one or two episodes of the *Andy Griffith*

Show. The divisiveness in our neighborhood recently reminds me of one particular episode from that series. Do you remember the one when Barney was cleaning out files and ran across a case that had never been closed? The case accused Floyd the barber of assault. It is hard to imagine Floyd raising his voice, much less assaulting anyone. Barney insisted that he would "get to the bottom of this" and marched down to the barbershop.

One interview led to another. Barney reported that Floyd had punched Charlie Foley in the face. Neither of them could remember why *until* Barney's dogged questions reignited the old conflict and the angry emotions.

Andy tried to convince Barney to let it go, but the damage was done. That afternoon, Floyd came in with a new black eye, followed by a long line of Mayberry's citizens also sporting black eyes, all with new assault charges to file. It's a typical Barney-chaos episode, but it resembles our neighborhood lately.

I appreciate that each of you is dedicated to your position and to our neighborhood. But I'd like you to reflect on the recent enthusiasm with which you have been enforcing rules and pursuing legal action. I think goodwill is as important as property values and ask you to think a little more about what Andy would do in this situation.

The "Barney" character in the room simply squinted in confusion and started to prattle the minute I stopped talking. But my target audience was the "Andys" in the room, who were naturally inclined to calm disputes rather than stir them up. They could see our local "Barney Fife" had gone too far.

Within the year, Barney was no longer president, and a mellower, wiser "Andy" was in place. We even had a pumpkin-carving party the next October.

PART 3

Perfecting the Craft

CHAPTER 11

Sensory Details Make Stories Experiential

EVEN IF YOU have never been to Russia, I can take you there with a story, using sensory experiences as building blocks to develop the scenery, characters, events, and consequences. I can use those building blocks to tell my story about seeing a Russian woman who appeared to be homeless, with tattered dresses and coats, selling small trinkets and handkerchiefs rather than begging for rubles. You already know what snow is. You have seen old ladies who are poor, and you have seen homeless people in big cities. If you have seen *Doctor Zhivago* (1965), you might use the train scene for the background. Sensory perceptions such as these are the building blocks of storytelling, and they come into play with my telling of this story:

In Russia, many old women have no safety net because the shift to a free market from communism was abrupt. It left millions of people who were subsidized all their lives

> without enough time to build up savings or assets. Anchor this with more sensory data: The woman burned into my memory stands in the freezing rain with as much dignity as she can, wearing an old crocheted sweater under her coat. The sweater was too fine to be warm and had one rhinestone button left. When I approached her to buy one of her handkerchiefs, her eyes were harder than I expected.

Now the real spin starts. Once I've created a mental image with added sensory details, I can cherry-pick more sensory details that are likely to generate emotions that her image might stir up in you: anxiety, despair, pity, or discomfort.

A Democrat from the United States might continue by saying that social security is vital to a free-market economy because otherwise people fall through the cracks. A Republican might emphasize how, over the years, government subsidies became so large they collapsed under the burden and left people trained to rely on the state, without skills or savings to support themselves in their old age.

Every story is spin; each story represents some subjective choice of which details are in and which are out. If you want your listeners to reach the same conclusions that you do, you need to create a story with the particular sensory experiences that create the perceptions you want to share with your listeners.

Surefire Sensory Associations

Urban legends display an array of emotional associations that are total fabrications but are educational nonetheless. What do these "stories" have in common? *NASA Experiments with*

Sex in Space; Nostradamus Predicted 9/11 Attack; Spiders under the Toilet Seat; Bill Gates to Share His Fortune; and the worst, *Young Cancer Victim Needs Your Help.* They all activate strong sensory imagination and strong emotions that momentarily override rational reasoning. The first time people hear that someone woke up in Las Vegas in a bathtub of ice missing a stolen kidney, they can almost feel the ice in the bathtub and see the handwriting on the note that tells them to call a hospital. Their imagination creates this experience well before their frontal lobes have a chance to challenge the plausibility of strangers harvesting kidneys by drugging hotel guests.

The "Spiders under the Toilet Seat" story is particularly interesting. It is a good example of a story that uses physiological triggers to travel. The author of this hoax used sensory details that were so vivid they bypassed rational thinking. The bites "happened" at an Olive Garden restaurant (specific—a place you know, even if you haven't been there) from a Two-Striped Telamonia (*Telamonia dimidiata*) spider (such a scientific-sounding name mimics validity). A realistic-sounding history provides a plausible back story: Several customers who became ill and later died had all dined at the same restaurant. One of them was a lawyer from Jacksonville who had returned from Indonesia (details familiar enough to inspire imagined visual images: lawyer, Jacksonville, Indonesia). He ultimately died from a puncture wound on his right buttock. The story invites your brain to connect the dots: hey, that spider must have hidden inside the guy's pants, bitten him, and crawled under the toilet seat when he was using the bathroom at the restaurant. I'm guessing very few people can read the original e-mail without flinching their right buttock muscle away from an imaginary spider bite. Once a story stimulates a

physical sensation in your listener's body and is accompanied
by a strong emotional experience, it has sticking power.

One of my heroes understands the power of stories to bring
numbers to life—audience analysis and high-level conceptualization are very important tools, but these abstractions don't
tell you what kind of sensory experiences create perceptions
and emotions. Economist Steven Levitt's book *Freakonomics* is
full of stories that use emotionally charged associations (e.g.,
"Why do crack dealers live with their mothers?" and "How are
real estate agents like the KKK?") to frame his numbers with
vivid images easily constructed in his readers' minds.[7]

Levitt is a master at stimulating sensory and emotional
sensations that correlate with the questions he asks and the
answers he finds. I heard him speak at a building-industry
conference. If possible, he is an even better storyteller in person than in his books. He began with what I might call an
I-Know-What-You-Are-Thinking story. This story demonstrates a reliably vibrant sensory hook: the fart. Notice how he
anchors his story with vivid and specific details.

> A recent survey of economists asks, "What is the most
> important skill for an economist?" Seventy percent answered,
> "A proficiency in math," and only 2 percent answered, "A
> good working knowledge of the economy." [*Pause for
> laughter.*]
>
> I am *not* good at math. I recently went to my high-
> school reunion and my math teacher, Mr. Drexel,
> remembered my name.

---

7. Steven Levitt and Stephen Dubner, *Freakonomics: A Rogue Economist
Explores the Hidden Side of Everything* (New York: HarperCollins, 2005).

He said, "Aren't you the one who got two out of five in calculus?"

I had to answer, "Yes."

Apparently, I got the lowest score of any of his students . . . ever. That's why he remembered me.

My first math class at MIT, I turned to a classmate and asked, "Hey, is there a difference between the curly *d* and the straight *d*?"

The guy just looked at me with pity and said, "You are in *so* much trouble, man."

I was so far behind my peers there was no way I could catch up. I wondered what to do, and then I remembered a story my father told me. When he was in medical school, his mentor took him aside. Apparently his aptitude wasn't so stunning either. His mentor told him, "Levitt, you don't have much talent for medical research. There are two ways you can go here. You could fight your way among the crowds of people who choose the most popular areas to research, or you can find an area where *no one* is researching and own it."

That is how my father decided to specialize in intestinal gas. In fact, he eventually became known as the "King of Farts." I took his words to heart and looked for my niche. *Freakonomics* is to traditional economics what intestinal gas is to traditional medicine.

Levitt starts with a sensory memory most of us share: high-school math. Listeners' memories flash a scene from their high-school math class, a guaranteed common experience in that crowd. The math teacher I remembered was Mr. Jackson. (Yours?) Levitt's story is endearing and preempts the audiences' expectations for him to display math-genius behaviors. He establishes his own antimath genre of economics as certainly more fun than—if not superior to—the egghead version. Describing his dad as the "King of Farts" uses past emotional, visual, auditory, and olfactory sensations that call out our inner kid, who is always willing to snicker at a fart reference. With this simple story, Levitt activated his audience's imagination, made his point, and guided expectations to match what he planned to deliver. It's much easier to satisfy expectations when you set them up to match what you intend to offer.

Levitt interacts with people as much as, or more than, with numbers. He is an active participant in real life. His curious explorations of the real lives of others supply him with stories that pop readily to mind whenever he needs to explain a concept. Those who never venture into the world don't have many stories to tell.

Experience Is Sensory

Audience analysis and high-level conceptualization are very important tools, but knowing your target's statistics (numerical abstractions) won't give you enough empathy to identify the specific sensory experiences that might lead to new perceptions. Storytelling uses the five primary channels through which we experience the world—what we smell, taste, hear, touch, and see—to simulate an influential experience. Sure, if you buy stock in a fluctuating market, a lone number can take you on a roller coaster of emotions, but only because of the physical associations you associate with an unusually high or low stock price: a luxury car versus a used junker, champagne versus beer, or retirement on a golf course versus a security guard job at the mall when you are eighty years old. It is what the number means in terms of the well-being of your body, spirit, and physical environment that stimulates emotions.

Full-Body Research

Simply identifying the age range and habits of your target audience is not enough. You only find stories after you shut off your computer, set aside the marketing research, and get out there and interact personally with the people you wish to influence.

If you want to ignite your creative intelligence, give your body and senses something to work with. Your brain may crave the false clarity of data, but only your body can take in the sights, sounds, smells, tastes, and feelings that stimulate emotions.

Personal experiences of what data mean in real life provide you with the details that will create a more visceral experience for your audience. You can literally create common ground by walking around in your audience's world and providing sensory clues that you see what they see. The credibility and creative ideas you reap from full-body research equip you with stories that connect and convince.

An article in the *New York Times* by William C. Taylor profiled the kind of research that finds stories.[8] A hedge fund,

---

8. William C. Taylor, "Get Out of That Rut and into the Shower," *New York Times*, August 13, 2006.

Second Curve Capital, focused on bank and financial services stocks by sending employees, analysts, compliance officers, computer geeks, and receptionists to the streets to do full-body research. For this "branch hunt," they were equipped with digital cameras, audio equipment, and crisp $100 bills to capture "flesh-and-blood experiences" of being a customer at banks and other financial institutions. Second Curve CEO Tom Brown's favorite story is about trying to open an account at a Chase bank and mentioning that he was switching from Citibank.

The Chase employee said, "I'm surprised you want to switch, I have my account at Citibank."

Brown says, "The biggest mistake companies make is managing to the averages. How long, on average, to open an account? What's the average level of customer satisfaction? Averages hide as much as they reveal."

As we discover through the art of storytelling, much of reality is hidden by averages and numbers. Only full-body research that results in "flesh-and-blood experiences" can produce vibrant stories. Any situation you seek to understand for purposes of influence or to gauge future actions is best researched in as physical a way as possible without preconceptions.

In Nigeria, I had the opportunity to ask for "stories" that women tell themselves about power. I told a story first, an English folktale called "Lady Ragnell" that ends by answering the riddle, "What do women want?" with the answer, "to choose for themselves." I then asked the women present to tell me a story about the last time they felt powerful. One woman told of having enough of her own money to lend a nephew $200 without asking permission from her husband. Another told of demanding that an arrogant doctor recheck the leg of a neighbor's child and remove the glass he had left to fester in the child's leg. A Muslim woman told of asking a school administrator who denied receiving a timely application she had personally delivered on behalf of a student to look at her face, against Muslim custom, and check again on his assertion that "he had never seen her." He had been holding the application back waiting for a bribe. She knew he was lying. She called him on it, and it left her feeling powerful that she prevailed. Numbers from a survey analysis of women in Nigeria would not—and could not—tell me what these personal experiences reveal.

Anyone who can't think of a story about their company culture or customers is spending too much time in their office.

Spending a week in a community plagued by diabetes without hiding behind a survey clipboard is bound to call into question faulty assumptions that educational brochures will improve eating habits. Any nutritionist would be forced to admit that brochures are never read and don't do a damn thing to change eating habits. If all medical researchers lived with their "population" for a week or more, we would see more innovations and fascinating stories, not to mention a heightened appreciation for those who research intestinal gas.

Often research is conducted on factors that are easy to isolate rather than factors that are most likely to change behavior. When subjective issues are prevented from "distorting" research, the results are stripped clean of the subjective context that really drives behavior. Evidence-based research may be accurate, but it misses innovative ideas that only come from firsthand observations of actual behavior.

There is always the risk that full-body research will debunk cherished assumptions, reveal flawed logic, and topple ivory towers. Sometimes stories take us backward so we can go forward. In Chapter 12, I discuss the potential for resistance that can erupt when stories embrace gritty realities rather than strive for best-case scenarios.

In the meantime, practice creating sensations in your stories by using familiar experiences and feelings—that is, get personal. If a story doesn't work on you, it probably won't work on others.

Exercise: Create Sensations

Practice creating sensations in your own mind to deepen your understanding of how words can activate the sensory areas of the brain.

In the interest of eliciting sensations that make your stories feel like real-life experiences, imagine a cutting board, and on that board, a juicy lemon warm from sitting in a sunny window. You can smell the oils of the zest. Imagine a very sharp knife and pick that knife up and cut the lemon in half. See the two halves rock away, and beads of lemon juice collect and then drip down into a puddle. Now you can smell the juice as well as the zest. Take one of the halves and cut it in half again. Pick up one of the quarters, bring it to your mouth, and bite deep; wrap your lips around it to make a big yellow smile, and let the juices run down your chin.

What happened? Did you feel your saliva glands tingle? Did your mouth water? That's because your imagination thought there really was a lemon. This is how a story works.

It activates the power of the imagination to simulate a real experience.

Your goal is to tell a story that activates the imagination of your listeners to see, hear, smell, touch, and taste (through imagination) your story as if it were really happening. That is vibrancy. Done well, your story may record in the brain as deeply as a real-life experience.

Set your story up to win by listing a set of vivid, stimulating descriptions for each of the five senses. You rarely use all the details you list, but the exercise always makes your story more vibrant in your mind. Imagining the details when you tell the story helps you viscerally reexperience the story as you tell it. If you don't see a story vividly unfold as you tell it, no one else will either.

But if you can see, hear, smell, touch, and taste your story as if it is happening in real time, your brain magically translates your tone, facial gestures, body movements, hand movements, timing, and word choice to build the scene in the imagination of your listeners. Tone, gestures, and timing flow effortlessly when your mind is reexperiencing the sights, sounds, taste, smells, and tactile sensations of your story.

CHAPTER 12

The Gift of Brevity

AS MUCH AS I'd like this chapter to be brief, brevity demands an enormous investment of time and energy. As Goethe put it in a letter to a friend, "If I had had more time, this would have been a shorter letter."

First, let's identify some root causes that undermine brevity. The opposites of brevity—waffling, droning, repetition, or other forms of boring an audience to death—occur because of predictable and avoidable issues that are best resolved before you tell a story. At the same time, editing too much or too soon in pursuit of the perfect "sound bite" or "elevator speech" can prune your story so severely that it can cripple its power to communicate.

What Is Your Story?

Brevity demands that you edit according to your own judgment about what is most important here and now. Trusting your judgment usually requires that you trust your audience, too. These tough choices become clear as you face the dilemma of choosing the stories that best tell who you are and why you are here. Choosing the highest outcome for your presentation is a rigorous process. Once you have resolved conflicting values and hidden dilemmas, editing for brevity is easy.

I once visited an old friend in the hospital. He and his wife were wealthy from a fitness equipment business, which they sold when he was diagnosed with Parkinson's disease. He was confined to a wheelchair, but his wife wanted to pretend nothing was wrong. She wanted to curb his spending on home care. She thought he didn't need a driver when she could drive and resented regularly buying new cell phones, thinking he could stop dropping them if he was more careful. I sat in the chair by his bedside, flooded with my own solutions to his problem. But they were *my* solutions.

You will sit in this chair someday if you haven't already. Someone you love, or someone who works for you, is a victim of unfair treatment, but you can't fix it for them. Only they can resolve the problem.

What does this have to do with brevity? The ambivalence of wanting to appear sympathetic and wanting to give someone a kick in the butt can trap you in a looping conversation. These loops cycle endlessly as new ideas are met with a "yes, but" rejection followed by sympathy, which elicits more examples of feeling trapped, which trigger new ideas for change, and you are back to "yes, but." It's an infinite loop that you can focus like a laser once you are willing to choose one value over another.

I was thinking, "You ought to have three phones at all times, because you are going to drop *all* of them. You have Parkinson's, fer crissakes."

But his depression frightened me, and I was very careful to put my needs aside and choose a story that met his needs. I chose a kick in the seat over sympathy, but once I chose I was free to do both. I told him this story:

> A law firm hired me to teach storytelling, and one of the young female lawyers told a story about her dad. He was a famous litigator. People said he "invented hardball litigation." But he wasn't such a great dad. One night she was talking on the phone, like any normal 15-year-old, and her father burst into the room. He grabbed the phone and slammed it down, berating her that he had been trying to call home for over 30 minutes. He yelled some more and then laid out a 10-minute maximum phone time and stormed out. We could see the hurt move across her face.
>
> Then she smiled and said, "Two weeks later, the phone company pulled up to our house to install my own private line. I called them myself and paid out of my own babysitting money. Problem solved."

Can you feel the brevity this story brings to what could otherwise be a preachy litany of positive thinking or "you poor dear" sympathy? After I told that story, I said, "If a 15-year-old can do it, so can you." And then I shut up. To talk more would have diluted the power of the story. I let him talk instead. The story did its work.

After crying about his wife's inability to make the transition to their new life, my friend put his fist in the air and said, "I'm not just getting another phone, I'm getting upgraded, too!"

Too Soon to Prune

Brevity is best sought after you are clear on the big issues. If you seek brevity from the beginning and look for the "sound bite" or the "elevator speech" from the get-go, you tend to think, "We don't have time for the Who-I-am, Why-I'm-here, What-is-the-highest-value bullsh**." After all, you are going to edit most of it out, aren't you? Perhaps, but removing the vegetables out of a good broth doesn't remove the flavors that remain.

In Chapter 11, I had you seeking mountains of sensory data you may not use, and this one asks deep, meaningful questions you may never mention directly in your telling. This is not a contradiction in advice; it is about a distillation process where you travel a particular sequence that refines complex issues and broad appeal into a powerful story. The breadth and depth of your investment shines through your story with brightness, intensity, and essence. It's like using a 100-watt bulb instead of a 30-watt bulb. Each bulb is the same size, turned on for the same three minutes, but one is more intense and its light reaches farther than the other.

Great artists and writers invest hours in search of an elegant expression or a single line that says it all. Picasso's original sketches possessed a remarkable realism that rivals photography, and yet his representations in later years edited out the realism and distilled an essence so intense that one painting can represent myriad levels of human experience. His painting *Guernica* brought me to tears in the same way the movie *Schindler's List* (1993) did. Consider the investment of time necessary to edit down to a few core details in one painting or one movie.

This is a good ratio for us to remember: millions of dollars and hours beyond reason are invested to create one experience. The painting that looks easy or the story that seems simple is often the product of many years of investment. Sure, there are times when the perfect story pops into your head, and you go with it. Most of the time, the perfect story is the product of flesh-and-blood experiences reported after self-examination and considered intention.

I love when friends call me to say, "I used a story and it rocked." Greg Fuson, a conference director, told me about a remarkably brief story that shows the kind of deep connection forged when you take the time to ask yourself, "Who am I? Why am I here? What is the highest outcome?"

> Greg walked onstage to introduce the first annual meeting of The Vine, a conference for developers who want to build social community, not just physical structures. In his arms, he held his baby daughter. He said, "I had the privilege of becoming a father twice this year—first my daughter, Anna, born seven weeks ago, and again today at the birth of this conference we are experiencing together. Being a father leaves me awestruck at the sense of responsibility I feel toward Anna: one human being taking care of another. I think the essence of community, in its purest form, is as simple as that: each one of us taking responsibility for the care of others."

That's brevity at its best. Take your longest story and ask yourself, "What is the central message I want to communicate?"

Practice Brevity

Most of your storytelling occurs during personal conversations, presentations, and informal interactions. This is the time to practice brevity. Try out various styles of editing when it doesn't matter so much so that you develop good habits for when it does matter. As you practice, you will discover the particular bugs in your system that hamper brevity: waffling due to internal conflicts, droning because you enjoy the sound of your own voice, excessive control needs, or lack of preparation. Most of these issues threaten us all at one time or another.

Begin by questioning everything you have been taught about how to sell ideas. Our larger culture, and your organizational culture, may have imposed formal and informal templates that pop into play when you set out to craft a story. These mental templates sometimes conflict. For instance, if you were taught to avoid ambiguity, you may convey so much certainty that you seem arrogant or incurious.

Be Subjective

Remember the agony of the dreaded meetings where we gathered to craft meaty statements of our companies' missions? We began with high expectations only to end up choosing words selected less on the promise of a bright future and more on the basis of ending the damn meeting. Then Scott Adams of *Dilbert* fame gave us access to David Youd's gag Automatic Mission Statement Generator, in which all you have to do is select a few key buzz words and out comes a tailor-made mission statement. In any culture where clarity reigns supreme, addressing subjective questions feels either ambiguous or oversimplified. Only stories and metaphor can approximate ambiguous concepts such as passion, service, and faith while maintaining participative input. As those "mission statement meetings" proved, wordsmithing goes on forever when a group seeks impossible levels of clarity.

Hidden assumptions about professional presentations and what is or is not appropriate can screw you up. If your mental template of "A Good Presentation" is a highly objective, linear progression, with all relative information presented in bullet points, you can end up with 70 slides that communicate less than a three-minute story does. Test yourself: If you were going to give a one-hour presentation on your most important project and its relevance to the organization's mission, what would it look like? Notice your mental to-do list. Does it start with time to reflect or opening PowerPoint to record a few bullet points?

I know one large organization where most presentations easily include an average of 70 PowerPoint slides, called a "deck." They spend hours formatting data and adding animation, images, and graphs. I doubt they realize the impact this presentation routine has on their thinking process. These hours feel like hard work and provide the illusion of improved communication. Performance anxiety can fill hours of formatting, sequencing, and display that would be better spent taking a walk first.

Brevity is better achieved by turning the computer off and asking yourself the basic questions. Who am I? Why am I here? What is the highest possible outcome of my presentation? This may not feel like real work because it involves a *lot* of staring into space, going for a walk, or even heading to the gym, but this is the work that builds a cohesive message. Be prepared for these questions to reveal incongruities, paradoxes, and conflicting values. That is exactly why you are taking the time to ask the questions. Unaddressed incongruities, paradoxes, and conflicting values are the root cause of waffling, superficiality, and too many details.

Imagine a human resources manager speaking to her company in a "town hall" meeting regarding a status report about customer service. This is a big topic with guaranteed paradoxes and incongruities. If customer service means the customer is always right, and yet the company also asserts, "People are our greatest asset," their stance is paradoxical. The human resources manager may be able to support both messages equally well with graphs, charts, and nice photos of customers and employees, but what is her story? Which one is it? If a mean customer treats an employee like dirt, what do you do? Do you protect your most valuable asset or tell the poor employee to suck it up because the customer is always right? This is the perfect place to tell a story about what is ultimately most important.

Take a Stand

Graphs tidy up reality, whereas stories reveal and help resolve the mess. Avoiding the messiness of reality is not the only way to be brief. Taking a stand achieves clarity, brevity, and the power of a clear, clean message. It requires that you both respect and trust your audience. And the minute you make that decision, it rearranges your presentation into a story that sticks, and it helps you edit your graphs and numbers down to the vital few. Knowing that employees always, in the end, come first as a way to achieve customer care is a powerful stand to make. It clarifies the priority of your core values. Core values always compete at some point. It takes courage to make the call, in advance, about which value you choose at the extremes when two values conflict.

Having the courage to make a tough call relieves your anxiety and the anxiety of an unresolved story. Knowing whether you value employees over customers, quality over quantity, or freedom over structure gives you power to pursue mutual goals. It resolves the ambiguity of your listener's reality into a meaningful story. It wins followers as well as enemies.

The brevity and clarity of a meaningful story reveals your personal feelings about an issue. Contrary to the "business isn't personal" myth, you have to have feelings before you can stimulate feelings in others. Trust, faith, passion, and empathy are ultimately personal, so your personal story makes the impersonal personal in as brief a time as possible.

CHAPTER 13

Storytelling by Committee

FINDING BIG STORIES to capture the essence of an organization, candidate, or brand is the Holy Grail for many newcomers to storytelling. They seek a brand or organizational story that packs an emotional punch and replicates and travels like a virus before they've learned good habits by practicing personal stories. They want a story that is simultaneously personal and collective, a story that sweeps attention and conclusions to a desired position.

After 9/11, the "freedom is on the march" story was powerful and motivating, and it was one of those stories that pre-interpreted all dissent as being "against us." It was a resilient enough story to contain contradictory data successfully. It created a metaphor that transformed news stories within the same frame: either winning or losing freedom. Complex truths take longer to communicate; they seemed to slow the march of freedom and thus translated to losing freedom.

While this story was running high, slower and more considered interpretations felt risky, even passive. Regardless of your politics, the "freedom is on the march" story worked its magic. But who chose this story? How did they choose it? What competing stories were also considered? Understanding the group-process dynamics of story creation and selection can be just as important as understanding the characteristics of a good story.

The quality of any story chosen to represent a group or agenda inevitably reflects the quality of the decision-making processes and thinking routines used by the group. If the group is disorganized and conflicted, the stories told are likely to be disorganized, conflicted, and weak. When a group is cohesive, deeply committed, open to risk, and disciplined in the face of adversity, they have a much better chance of divining a story that pulls from the universal well of meaning.

Borrowing from the language of myth, these bigger stories are archetypal stories that trigger deep, personal recognition because they highlight universal patterns of experience/response that draw attention, bring meaning, and create a sense of belongingness. Fear is a very strong universal pattern. Urban myths demonstrate the stickiness of fear stories. Love, hope, and faith stories seem to need more energy, imagery, and even self-discipline to travel as far as fear stories.

Managing group progress by adhering to a strict taxonomy or formulaic definition of "story" only gives you the illusion that you are tapping into the magic of the collective creativity and insight of your group. A formula cannot teach you how to create group consensus without the normal process losses of people who talk too much, too little, and so on. If you as an individual produce the perfect story, you still have to convince everyone else on the team that your story is "It."

Understanding the predictable dynamics of group process helps you navigate waves of emotion that push, pull, and tumble story ideas. Great stories often lose cohesion and magic by the time they are approved by a committee.

Creativity and Deviance

When I was in advertising, our creative team often mourned "magic" stories that were picked clean of all their magic by nervous product managers measuring and evaluating subjective metaphors with objective criteria. They often responded to a story by weighing worst-case scenarios of misinterpretation against unproven gains, wary of distinctive images.

I remember our creative team pitched a radio ad to capitalize on Ford's sponsorship of the Australian Open in 1994 by using tennis court sounds in the background as well as the trademark sound effect of Monica Seles's grunt as she hit the ball. Because Monica Seles had won the Australian Open in 1991, 1992, and 1993, and because Australians love their sport, we were confident radio listeners would easily recognize her trademark grunt. But the product manager had reservations. He became fixated on the potential for listeners to find the grunt unpleasant in some way. The creative team narrowed their eyes, and one leaned forward and asked, "Unpleasant how, exactly?" Lines were drawn, and while civility and "the customer is always right" language prevailed, the "story" of performance with "grunt" died in that room without a funeral.

That radio spot may or may not have had the magic we thought it did, but its death on the cutting room floor had less to do with the value of the story and more to do with the power struggles between the individuals making the decision.

Often, creative ideas initially appear deviant because they are. A favorite story about this struggle comes from 1978, supposedly in the Coca-Cola boardroom. The marketing and advertising gurus were struggling over the decision to name a new lemon/lime soda they planned to introduce the next year. The favorite name of the creative team was "Mello Yello."

When the product manager finally articulated his reservations, he said, "Mello Yello just . . . sounds like the name of a street drug." To which the creative director nearly leapt across the table to ask, "What in the hell do you think Coke is?"

Objective thinkers seem to think that reducing ambiguity is the same as reducing risk—not so. Ambiguity reflects real life, so it makes a story feel real. Retaining the ambiguity and then testing a story in a low-risk experiment is a much better way to minimize risk in storytelling. In fact, Chapter 16 profiles how Coca-Cola so dramatically changed the methods used to test story ideas that they had to redistribute their marketing budget.

When Metrics Don't Help

Choosing the right story depends equally on your group's imagination and your group's skill in making subjective decisions. Groups in the unfamiliar territory of images, metaphor, and emotion often seek relief by oversimplifying these immeasurable qualities and converting them into some kind of quantifiable criteria. This default to numbers doesn't make for a better story; it just allows for an easier decision.

Another escape route is to lean too heavily on the opinions of the most powerful people in the group. This dependence strategy works just fine if that person is a brilliant storyteller. Having a genius storyteller at your helm is an ideal situation. Genius leaders such as Martin Luther King Jr., Henry Ford, and Steve Jobs have delivered stories that move huge groups of people to actions that turn vision into reality. However, most of us nongeniuses are stuck in committees with other nongeniuses, struggling with paradoxes, competing values, and diversities that swell and shrink our sense of cohesion on all big decisions, including "What is our story?" These are the groups sorely tempted to default to data sets, rules, and algorithms in order for their decisions to be more "rational."

In her book *On Becoming an Artist*, Ellen Langer cites research into the "illusion of control" as she ruthlessly deconstructs our favorite habits of using set principles and cognitive frames to improve decisions.[9] Particularly in business, routines that make decisions easier may sacrifice the engaging messiness of human experience. The better we get at acting like automatons, the less meaningful our stories become.

There are no magic formulas. All the really important issues in life are ambiguous and subjective. Your definition of success depends on your culture, age, socioeconomic status, personality, and recent life events. I've seen many groups locked in mortal combat, as if there were a "right" answer. Subjective issues have many "right" answers. To find a story that makes your target market feel important depends on where you and they are, who you and they are, when you and

---

9. Ellen J. Langer, *On Becoming an Artist: Reinventing Yourself through Mindful Creativity* (New York: Ballantine, 2005).

they are, why you seek to engage them, and why they might want to respond. Whether you chose the answers to these questions or they were chosen for you, you must find your own meaning from your point of view.

Statistics answers some of our questions. However, once we begin to select and test story ideas in focus groups, in test campaigns, or simply by running them up the flagpole, it is important to stay aware that everything from this point on is a result of subjective choices *based on the questions asked.* I don't mean to degrade the value of research, but it is important to resist the urge to treat research results like "facts." In this subjective milieu, the single most important piece of advice I can offer is to stay personally involved. Today, iterative testing is replacing the kind of qualitative research that tests pieces of a story in favor of the whole.

Storytelling as a Self-Diagnostic Process

In order to tell you a story that communicates who I am and why I am here, I must spend a little time asking myself those questions. This is usually done at a superficial level and as quickly as possible: "We manufacture electronics that entertain people and earn a profit for our company." Snore.

Self-examination is difficult enough at the individual level, but at the group level, egos get involved, old disagreements surface, and ideological differences can turn adults into kids fighting over the front seat. My friend Jim Signorelli gathers executives in a structured process as he presents 12 archetypes identified by Carol Pearson (wanderer, warrior, magician, etc.), and he asks them to individually select the one or two they feel fits best as a brand story.[10] The dialogue begins as people relate the meaning they see in their selections. The conversations that follow operate as a collective search for who we are (and are not) and why we are here.

This self-diagnostic process scares the hell out of people who aren't sure they are living meaningful lives. That's because the process of self-examination can test your faith that your organization and your group are basically good people with good intentions who walk their talk. Groups that avoid deep examination seem anxious that honest self-examination might expose hypocrisy or emptiness, but that is an important finding if you are looking for a compelling brand or organizational story. Anxiety flares when objective, outside-in thinking tools are set aside for subjective, inside-out thinking tools. I've found that anxiety tends to be overstated in most cases. Once a group is willing to reflect, most people find that their lives and work are full of meaning.

I prefer to begin by asking individual members of the group to tell a story that expresses who they are and why they are here, personally. Sharing these stories minimizes nitpicking later because it demonstrates the difficulty of trying to communicate big concepts such as "who we are" and "why we are here." It improves the process when everyone understands how deep and how personal the roots of an organization's Vision story need to be.

First attempts at group stories are often highly aspirational in that the story is more likely to tell who they wished they were rather than who they are. Stories that aspire to more than

---

10. Jim Signorelli, *Storybranding 2.0: Creating Stand-Out Brands through the Purpose of Story* (Austin, Tex.: Greenleaf, 2014).

you can back up sound hypocritical. It's OK to want to be better than you are, but Who-We-Are and Why-We-Are-Here stories should not promise more than you can deliver. I heard a minister once define hypocrisy as "a 14-year-old boy standing in the balcony holding his girlfriend's hand and singing, 'All that thrills my soul is Jesus.'" If there is some sense that "who you are" isn't who you say you are, then you have other issues to fix before you tell your story.

True faith in your organization is based in honesty. Since the Internet has increased transparency anyway, you may as well use storytelling to better match reality with aspirations. The process of self-diagnosis through storytelling forces your group to keep their eyes wide open while gathering stories that both fuel and douse that faith. Embrace *all* the stories—even the stories that represent less-than-ideal aspects of your organizations. The level of reality you embrace translates to authenticity in the stories you eventually choose to tell.

Solidarity Is Inside-Out

Stories that mobilize active engagement trigger personal recognition: that's me, this is about my life, this impacts people I love. Belongingness and solidarity are response and cause. Too often, belongingness is sought by matchy-matchy strategies that—with images of race, adopted jargon, and other imagined hooks—try to tie you to a particular demographic and say, "This is you." The problem with this approach is that it is an "outside-in" rather than an "inside-out" approach. Find stories that suggest we are the same, and you find a mutual connection. Our "outsides" will always be different. But as human beings, our "insides" share common elements that can leap across superficial distinctions to connect at a much deeper level: the level at which myth operates or, as Jung might call it, the collective unconscious.

The myth of Eris, the goddess of discord, is a good example. Most people have at one time or another personally experienced this kind of situation:

> Invitations to an upcoming wedding omitted the goddess Eris. All the gods and goddesses wanted to have a good time, and Eris caused trouble. So they omitted her name from the invitation list. Eris showed up anyway. She threw a golden apple that was engraved "For the Fairest" into the middle of the room. The catfight that resulted among Hera, Athena, and Aphrodite completely ruined the wedding. It ultimately led to the Trojan War when Paris awarded the apple to Aphrodite after she promised him the love of "the fairest of all women," Helen of Troy.

All groups deal with dissent. They may try to escape dissent, but the goddess of discord visits any meaningful group with big decisions to make. This dissent will come invited or uninvited. The advantage of inviting dissent intentionally is that your story can become more robust as result of the turmoil. Stories with enough collective meaning to tolerate disagreements inside the group can tolerate differences outside the group as well.

You and I are not gods or goddesses (except on weekends, maybe), yet we recognize the Eris story as both personal and collective. But I hope you can relate to Eris and her apple.

We've all lived this story. Sometimes we were the ones who avoided "trouble." Sometimes we were the trouble. I began using the word *solidarity* more often after I read the following quote by Eduardo Galeano: "I don't believe in charity. I believe in solidarity."

Charity is like flattery. It is vertical and flows from judgment. Solidarity is horizontal and more connected. When a group pursues solidarity instead of image, it demands more and delivers more powerful stories. A group that finds their organizational story from among stories they have gathered personally builds their ability to synchronize internal passions with external passions. To sit in someone else's chair or to walk a mile in his shoes: this is the kind of research that produces stories that makes customers, employees, or donors feel important again.

CHAPTER 14

Point of View

TRULY INFLUENTIAL STORYTELLING comes from the ability to step into and out of different points of view. This is a matter of developing your ability to jump through time and space so you can "see" your story from multiple points of view. This is a skill that will improve your storytelling in two ways: First, you can find a point of view from which to respect just about any audience. Your listeners will hear this respect in your voice, and you will smooth even the most ruffled fur. Second, you can re-view your most important stories from different points of view. This process richly develops details and depth that change your story from being one dimensional to having three- or even six-dimensional vibrancy, and it invites understanding from many different perspectives.

Looking at multiple points of view gives you more opportunity to feel what your audience feels and see what they see. The goal is to intentionally be less objective and more personal. Only a personal connection can generate the empathy that causes others to reciprocate in kind. This is impossible to sustain if you don't like or respect your audience. The primary stumbling block that sabotages most attempts to influence others is a lack of respect for or trust in the people you are trying to influence.

People can tell when you don't respect them. The clues are tiny but impossible to hide. Political conversations are a good time for observing how politeness fails to hide disrespect. Even family members, who love and respect each other deeply most of the time, can disrespect each other and destroy their opportunity to connect across divisive topics.

Tone, facial expressions, and body language will always give away the story you are telling yourself about your audience. If a middle manager gives a report to senior management, secretly thinking they are a bunch of idiots and that his or her presentation will be futile, chances are the presentation will be futile. These nonverbal communications may never reach the presenter's or senior management's awareness, but negative feelings distort interpretations. Most presentations of vital importance are between two groups that harbor secret stories that discount or discredit the other. Senior managers may think some workers join unions to exploit that power and compensate for failed careers. School teachers think the principal is really a pawn. The CEO thinks board members are already biased. There are a thousand stories out there that leave you feeling "right" but keep you from being connected.

Is Bias Bad?

Bias isn't good or bad. Bias is unavoidable. Your body can only be in one place at a time, and you have lived in a certain time and place that created your perceptual frame. The fad of using objective thinking to "remove bias from decision making" may have led you to believe that unbiased decisions are possible. Objective decision-making tools encourage you to remove or ignore bias as if, once removed from the decision-making process, bias will go away. Bias doesn't disappear. It simply continues to frame interpretations without your input. Ignored bias, personal feelings, and emotional reactions can dramatically sabotage the success of "unbiased" decisions. Since there are no emotionless environments, it's a good idea to investigate relevant sources of bias and learn what conclusions these points of view produce.

In the same way that no person can experience life without bias, no story is without bias. A story without bias is boring because it becomes disembodied, sterilized, and dehumanized. Behavior is always based on some point of view, so own it and demonstrate that you aren't blind to (or blinded by) your personal bias.

The answer is to narrate different points of view. Include details that provide evidence that you know and understand other points of view. By practicing shifting points of view, you will enrich your storytelling and your ability to read a room. One fun example comes from Gregory Maguire, who decided to tell the story of the *Wizard of Oz* from the Bad Witch's point of view. He ended up with a new book, *Wicked: The Life and Times of the Wicked Witch of the West*, and a successful Broadway musical. There is no telling what can happen when you develop this amazing skill.

Point of view alters meaning, but, more important to you, point of view also *creates* meaning. Choosing a time, place, and point of view from which to tell a story is what makes a story feel like a real experience. Using your story to travel through time and space can demonstrate how many equally valid points of view you see. Remember the story in Chapter 1 about the farmer and his horse? Each day's experiences reframed whether finding the horse was lucky or unlucky. There is nothing right or wrong with these shifting points of view. Since our bodies are subject to time and space, the only way to experience life is from a subjective point of view. The trick is to learn how to mentally and emotionally transport yourself into other points of view. By learning what others know, seeing what others see, and connecting to others, you earn the right to ask them to visit your point of view as well.

Here is a simple example:

1. *Objective point of view*: Employee X's attendance is down 25 percent, and performance levels indicate two missed deadlines.

2. *Employee X's point of view*: A staff member tells you that Employee X recently lost his three-year-old child in a drowning accident in the family's backyard pool and that he and his wife are getting a divorce.

3. *Staff's point of view*: Most of your staff have been saving up their own vacation time to donate to Employee X to help him take more time off.

Objectively, you might be justified in firing this person. However, from at least two subjective and humane points of view, you would risk your entire team's morale and might earn a new reputation as a heartless monster. Examining important decisions by using stories from several points of view can save you a lot of grief. You can avoid hurt feelings and time-wasting resentments if you take the time to examine your most important stories from several points of view.

Exercise: Examine Alternate Points of View

It might be interesting to take a Vision story and rewrite it twice from the point of view of two other characters. First, pick a nonhero from your story and retell the story from the beginning to the end from that character's point of view. You can't learn too much about telling a Vision story better.

Next, write the story again from the point of view of someone who "loses" something in your original version of the story. For example, one of my Vision stories in Chapter 8 was about Galileo and how he managed to continue to tell his truth and avoid burning at the stake for it.

I chose to research and reimagine Galileo's story from the pope's point of view. Every time Galileo spouted his heresies, the pope was losing control over the church's dogma and potentially, from his point of view, losing souls. As a result of rethinking this story, I began to see that, like many leaders, the pope may have agreed with Galileo but had an obligation to keep peace in his organization. The organization wasn't ready to incorporate this new truth without losing credibility. Seeing this point, I am able to use this story to facilitate understanding in fractious situations where bosses and heretics come to empathize with the good intentions of the other. This story can reach organizational leaders in a way that validates their power while, at the same time, it points to the possibility of peaceful collaboration. This is cool stuff.

Write your story from a "loser's" point of view. Choose any character who, in your Vision story, might end up feeling as if he or she lost status, power, autonomy, or something else of value. Ham it up and give yourself over to his or her point of view. This is a creative exercise, so have some fun with it.

This exercise should have proven one of two possible alternatives: either your Vision story can be told inspirationally from several points of view or—and you need to know this—your Vision story is motivating only for you. "Hero" Vision stories often feed the ego of the teller more than the needs of the group. Using this exercise will save you from making a mistake. Having a strong ego is vital in taking a leadership role. Keeping that ego in check is equally vital to those who must decide whether they want to follow your leadership.

Use this exercise any time one of your stories isn't working. You may discover that your story, or your telling of it, unintentionally disregards the point of view of someone vital to your success.

CHAPTER 15

Story Listening

I

T'S AMAZING HOW unaware we can be of the stories that run our lives. Whether your story is that "life is like a box of chocolates" or that "life is a bitch and then you die," you carry your beliefs around in the form of stories and metaphors. If you really want to tell stories that win, first identify and then listen to these stories and metaphors that frame your own reality.

You need to know where you are in order to meet people where they are.

Examine the stories embedded in your mind and environment. You can't wallpaper a story of hope, trust, and integrity onto disillusioned, stressed-out, and cynical stories. The new stories peel right off again, like water-based paint on enamel.

Mapping the Mental Terrain

One critical story that can affect your (anyone's, really) ability to listen is the story that defines your hopes for the future.

By *hope*, I mean how positively you view the gap between the current reality and what you see as desirable and plausible in the future. Whether you intend to make a presentation, give a sales pitch, or ask for donations, this core story plays in the background to shape your dialogue.

Stop and ask yourself, "Is my story about hope?" Does your story paint hope as naive? Or does your story about hope help you get up in the morning? Before you make another presentation about a future project, I recommend you stop and listen to the stories that are operating right now in your mind and in your audience's minds.

This process feels awkward. Asking coworkers out of the blue, "Tell me a story about hope," is a bit weird. It's better if you lay some groundwork. Give them a reasonable basis for the question. For example, say, "I'm trying to get a fix on how we approach projects, and I need your help. This doesn't have to apply to your job, but how would you characterize our willingness to risk in pursuit of extraordinary outcomes?"

Be prepared to stay silent when they give you strange looks. Steer them away from hypothetical or existential discussions. Keep asking for a concrete example. Ask them for a story. If necessary, tell your own story about a recent or important experience of hope or hopelessness. Don't force your story or theirs to move in the direction you would prefer—that will give you a false reading. Don't try to craft the story in any way. This is a process of mapping the mental terrain. You don't draw maps based on where you wish the mountains were. Useful maps show where the mountains actually are.

After you understand the currents and riptides currently governing perceptions, you are better equipped to dive in and focus on desired outcomes. Mapping the mental terrain by listening to currently active stories opens up your focus and stops you from being too tightly directed toward desired outcomes. Before you focus on the stories you want people to believe, it helps to see what stories they already believe. Understanding current stories and allowing yourself to be influenced by them will build your story in a way that taps into or redirects the most important rivers of meaning. The key is not only to hear these stories but to let them do their work on you. This may unravel carefully constructed plans, but better now than later.

Listening for Stories

Great artists seek out art. Great chefs like to eat the food of other excellent cooks. Writers read voraciously. If you love it, you seek it out. For those who love storytelling, listening is easy. Great storytellers are compulsive story listeners.

But what if you don't love storytelling? Perhaps instead of listening to stories, you would rather read a magazine or listen to music. Storytelling and story listening are not going to be everyone's favorite pastimes.

It's not the quantity of listening as much as the quality of listening that counts, but describing that quality is tricky. While training courses in active listening may teach you the pragmatics of holding eye contact, nodding, leaning forward, paraphrasing back, and making reassuring noises, they don't teach you to actually listen. They teach us how to fake listening. One time when I made that joke, a Hungarian woman in the back of the room raised her hand and said in a Zsa Zsa Gabor accent, "Yes! Listening is just like sex." I jumped right in, "How so?" She replied, "Ven ze desire is there, ze skills will follow." She's got a point.

Most people don't listen because they have other things they'd rather do. They are so focused on their own needs, quelling anxiety, or moving into action that they literally can't listen. They are so keen to speak that they can't hear.

I remember a chief of staff at a hospital who challenged the idea that his listening style had anything to do with it. He said, "I ask people all the time to tell me what's going on, and they sit there mute like bumps on a log."

His impatient tone and the metaphor he used to describe staff—"bumps on a log"—betrayed the low quality of listening this otherwise well-intentioned man offered his staff. I teased him by pointing out that if he engaged in some of the watch checking, facial gestures, overtalking, or other cues he was currently displaying, it could have trained his staff that despite his questions, he only wanted to hear agreement. He was grumpy for a while, but, by the end of the day, he had set his sights on changing the results by changing his listening style.

The Opposite of Listening

Someone once told me, "Listening is the period of time I must wait until I get to speak again." At least he was being more honest with himself than Dr. Bump-on-a-Log.

If you are bothered by internal "B.S. Alerts," "Whacko Alerts," or "Jerk Alerts," it means you have stopped listening to the speaker and have begun to slice, dice, categorize, and judge the speaker's words, intentions, and meaning. Threatened by the uncertainty of listening, you might react with sarcasm; ridicule is an excellent way to avoid listening. We all do it at one time or another. Whether your face correlates to your internal critique or you have mastered the poker face, the damage is done. This is a natural reaction when you listen to people you wish to influence because you are engaging someone with opinions you wish to alter. Yet the listening part of your influence process requires you to listen closely to stories even when they contradict your own. Holding your story at bay while you fully experience others' points of view without judgments is the key to real listening.

Our world moves so fast that we are pressured to make sense of incoming data as quickly as possible. Speed and focus have become unquestioned values applied to communication. People mindlessly try to improve communication by increasing speed and focus. That's great when you seek only to inform. However, when you seek to influence, speed and focus narrow the bandwidth across which you communicate. Narrow connections produce less influence. Listening is slow and wide rather than fast and narrow. It is sort of like cleaning up a mess faster with a heap of towels applied in a slow, wide sweep rather than with one towel quickly rubbed back and forth. Mindless speed and focus are the culprits of most bad communication. If you rush past conflicting elements, you may miss the leverage point that would change minds. If you rush past what people find hard to express, you lose opportunities to understand what drives them.

You might wonder, isn't listening all *about* focus? Aren't you focusing on the person telling the story? Well, yes and no. It depends on why you are focusing and how you are focusing. If your focus is wide and receptive—if you are willing to allow their words to change how you think—then yes, that's the kind of focus that draws true feelings and meaningful stories out of people. However, if you focus only on finding weakness or opportunities to distort, exploit, or contradict, then you could use a little help.

True Listening

True listening is a function of being present to other people's words and meaning, especially when their words and meaning might potentially refute or destabilize your own. It's easy to listen to someone who thinks the way you think, but you don't need extra help influencing people who think like you do. Listening to those who don't think like you is what earns you the right to hear and retell powerful stories that build connections. When you understand another's story so well you can retell it with its meaning intact, your retelling provides evidence that you value his or her opinion. If you don't take the time to do this, the person is likely to decide that you don't have anything to say that he or she will value in return.

The kind of listening that earns you a turn telling your own story is the kind that requires you to stay connected to another person's point of view despite seemingly irreconcilable differences, at the expense of temporarily setting your own point of view aside. Listening in this way can almost feel like surrender.

Is Listening Dangerous?

It can be. I read somewhere that if anyone ever listened to the whole story of any one woman's experience, the universe would crack in two. For me, this metaphor expresses the idea that true empathy with the universal forces of maternal joy, love, and suffering would deconstruct the barriers we erect around commerce and government. Listening to stories means staying present to collective human experiences of wonder and atrocity. My friends who work with HIV/AIDS research, in social services, and in other types of community work have learned that good listening requires boundaries. If you do nothing but listen to sad stories, you might drown in sorrow and hopelessness. The line of people ready to tell you stories about bad things is much longer than the line of people waiting to tell you stories about good things.

Sometimes, I see people who are action focused and who treat real, fully engaged listening as much too risky for forward progress. It is true that genuine listening can mean ceding control and risking manipulation or exploitation.

Listening is not something you do all the time or without end. It is a choice based on what you can process and how important it is for you to make a connection. It's not like handing the keys to your brain over to a stranger. You are still in charge. True, genuine listening *feels* risky when time is short, but you don't abdicate decision making just because you slow down long enough to imagine another person's experiences. Listening may take you to a place you don't want to go. Listening may reveal trouble about which you were blissfully ignorant. Still, listening always makes you smarter and earns you stronger connections to work with and through.

Good boundaries, and a solid sense of who you are and why you are here, give you the stability and stamina to find the stories that reveal the core values and beliefs of those you wish to influence. You may have to surf over looping repetitions, blue sky perkiness, and a few angry tirades, but eventually the waves of meaning will appear as patterns both to you and, possibly for the first time, to them.

Ending at the Beginning

Whether you spend your time gathering stories or telling stories, the skills are reciprocal. If you think, "I don't have any stories to tell," you invalidate yourself and the people around you. Listen for stories. They are all around you. Go on a scavenger hunt for stories and you will find them. Finding stories is best done in personal, face-to-face conversation. Forms and surveys are impersonal and predetermined by the questions they ask. Get out there and do some full-body research. Don't send someone else to find your stories for you. Finding stories is its own reward.

Often, people don't recognize how their life experiences can become incredibly compelling stories. If it was meaningful to you, it can be meaningful to others—if you tell the truth. Stories that are cleaned up are not as interesting as untidy, but more human, stories. If you don't have a high tolerance for imperfection, people will shy away from telling you the "whole story." And it's common wisdom that the rest of the story is where you find the most interesting bits.

One time, I heard someone complain that her story was boring, so I automatically replied, "Then you need to tell the truth." She responded, "Do you mean the part when I had an affair with the minister?" That certainly didn't sound very boring to me. If you dig a little deeper, you usually find a story of interest. I read somewhere that in order for people to seem interesting, you have to be interested in people.

My friend and story coach Doug Lipman taught me the phrase "Listen with delight." I recommend it to you: Listen with delight and the expectation you will learn something important. If you do that, you will have plenty of wins from both storytelling and story listening.

CHAPTER 16

Borrowing Genius

SOME OF THE brightest minds in their fields have aggressively applied storytelling principles, applications, and practices to their own goals with great effect. They now offer more practical insights, creative applications, and experiments than do many so-called storytelling experts. This chapter outlines some of their most innovative applications, along with ideas on how to transplant them into your own practice of personal storytelling.

Secrets of the Design-Thinking Process: User Stories

I used to love teaching storytelling to scientists and engineers because there was so much low-hanging fruit. In many cases, there still is. However, design engineers ate that low-hanging fruit years ago. They took storytelling and ran with it. My first hint came 10 years ago when I worked with some brilliant design engineers, including Xbox designers. They just nodded when I made distinctions between objective and subjective thinking. I called it story thinking, but they already had a name: design thinking.

Today, designers, information architects, and software developers begin projects by gathering stories about users' experiences that track unconscious preferences, map emotional reasoning, identify pockets of solutions that might scale, and track a user's journey in time and space. Andrew Hinton (andrewhinton.com), an information architect, describes his personal journey from data to story.

> This work, more than any other I'd done before, taught me that stories aren't merely an extra layer we add to binary logic and raw data. In fact, it's reversed—the stories are the foundations of our lives, and the data, the information, is the artificial abstraction. It's the dusty mirror we use to reflect upon ourselves, merely a tool for self-awareness.

Deborah J. Mayhew, a pioneer in user-interface design, describes what it was like back in the 1980s: "Engineers trained in and fascinated by formal logic were designing user interfaces for people with no similar training or interest." Today, designers can build a more realistic model of users' informal logic by gathering stories into a user-journey map.

Why not borrow user experience to design your next presentation? The first step is to gather user stories. This is not the same as analyzing your audience. Demographics, titles, and summarized goals cannot capture emotional and situational complexities or a true story heard firsthand. For instance, a group determined to decrease childhood obesity spent enough time asking kids to tell them stories about a time when exercise was fun that they ditched their plan to design a tracking device stimulated by music. Instead, they designed a much more social game device that facilitated interaction based on activity.

Design engineers also use templates to describe requirements in the terms of a user story: "As a (type of user) I want (goal) so that (reason why)."

While these user stories are currently very technical, notice that this template actually asks for three of the six stories addressed in this book, "Who are you? Why are you here? What is your vision?" The format demands we temporarily set our agendas aside in order to truly understand stories as personal as Who-I-Am, Why-I-Am-Here, and Vision stories. If we only hunt for stories to prove our point, it narrows our opportunities, creates blind spots, and stunts creative thinking.

I often ask permission to interview a cross section of staff, including people from the field, before I work with a team. Field staff tell very compelling who/why stories. If I am lucky, I find a story that delivers an insight not yet seen from a leader's point of view. Phone interviews begin with probing questions such as "I want to understand your role better. Could you tell me what your typical day looks like?" This anchors the conversation with real experiences instead of summarized opinions such as "I'm busy all day." More questions such as "When did you last feel truly proud of your work?" or "What can you tell me about your best/worst day?" keep the conversation going so I can gather good details in case I share these stories later: "Who was there? What year was this?" or "Where was this particular meeting held? What kind of room is that?"

Connecting a person to sensory details evokes true stories of real experiences that are more authentic and informative than summaries or conclusions. These stories help me design workshops that are more "user friendly." When I share true stories that mirror experiences familiar to my audience, it makes training more interesting, more memorable, and often more valuable. The discipline of designing how you communicate from the standpoint of creating a satisfying user's/student's/boss's/peer's experience (story) improves just about any type of communication.

Some design engineers go far beyond interviews to gather stories. The design firm IDEO offers a free toolkit on Human-Centered Design for nonprofits (www.ideo.com/images/uploads/hcd_toolkit/IDEO_HCD_ToolKit.pdf) in which it suggests gathering stories in individual and group interviews. But it goes further to suggest immersing yourself in the user environment so you have your own stories to share. You can ask users to self-document with photos, images, or words and even facilitate a community-driven discovery process. When the stakes are high, there is no better way to gather stories than to take a walk in their shoes or participate with users in some kind of discovery process.

In Chapter 5, I shared a story about facilitating a "Photo-Story" project in a poor Houston suburb. We handed out disposable cameras and asked people to take photos of images that told the story of their community. This act of self-documentation stimulated a community-driven discovery process that provided true stories and amazing images that were far more compelling than any story I might have told. I also learned more about underserved populations than I could have learned any other way. Granted, there was a lot more to it than passing out cameras, but if you want stories, I highly recommend immersing yourself in your audience's physical environment and collaboratively finding emotionally significant stories that inform and facilitate communication.

Secrets of the Design-Thinking Process: Solution and Story Testing

We know that focusing on problems, particularly perceptual problems such as bad morale, can make things worse rather than lead to solutions. User-experience designers confirm this and take it a step further. Understanding your audience means looking for user stories of solutions as well as stories about the problem. No matter how great my ideas may seem to me, it is just as likely there are users who have created solutions that might work better. It is pretty easy to find out. A quick turnaround between finding stories and testing these stories and solutions with real users saves wasting time on intermediate feedback from focus groups or surveys designed to predict success. Why wait? Steve Jobs famously distrusted focus groups in favor of direct observation and experiments. The iPhone innovation of using the index finder as a pointer is a great example of leaping over analysis and following stories of direct observation with experiments.

In a marketing plan for "liquid content," Coke virtually eliminated the kind of preliminary qualitative research they normally conducted on advertising ideas and shifted that money and time to "inspirational spaces," finding and testing stories that can be expressed in "every possible connection" that are "so contagious [they] cannot be controlled." (See the video "Content 2020" at www.youtube.com/watch?v=fiwIq -8GWA8.) Rather than running tests that might predict the success of a story idea, Coke shifted that budget to real tests of stories told to/by real consumers. Coke set up a perpetual, community-driven discovery process that generates and gathers customer stories so they can invest in the best stories that reinforce their "Coke is happiness" story. If the story works, it works. If not, they move on. The term "iterative testing" and the phrase "fail fast and often" are core principles for design thinking.

The problem with root cause analysis is that it often reveals root causes that are beyond our ability to influence, and while relevant, they are not helpful for finding solutions. For instance, in the case of malnourished children, the root causes include poverty, famine, and corruption, but these problems aren't going away tomorrow. Jerry Sternin from Save the Children (profiled in *Switch* by Chip and Dan Heath[11]) didn't chase root causes but rather chased solutions by collecting stories about the few inexplicably well-nourished kids in the same part of Vietnam suffering from widespread malnutrition. It turned out that the mothers of these kids told stories of feeding their kids "adult food" of tiny, protein-rich shrimp from rice patties and sweet-potato greens that other mothers considered low class. Sternin created a time and place for mothers to share their stories firsthand. He didn't interpret their stories for them. He knew that emotion- and context-rich stories lose something in translation. Solution-based stories not only deliver an emotionally significant story, but they

---

11.   Chip Heath and Dan Heath, *Switch: When Change Is Hard* (New York: Random House, 2010).

also become Teaching stories that create and expand solutions. The mothers' stories dramatically improved nutrition in the region.

Likewise, 10 years ago, the smart people at Dove (soap) immersed themselves in users' and customers' points of view across 10 countries to learn that only 2 percent of women felt beautiful. Dove didn't attack the root causes of feeling ugly but instead began sharing solution-based stories via its "Campaign for Real Beauty." It posted billboard images of beautiful, "normal-sized" women and invited women to share their own stories of real beauty. The result was a dramatic increase in market share and deep levels of engagement.

How did Dove know posting beautiful pictures of naked women with realistic bodies would engage women to feel more beautiful and tell their own stories? How could Save the Children know mothers would start cooking shrimp and greens for their children? They didn't. They simply told the stories and let their audience respond (or not).

Dove put up billboard-sized pictures of beautiful women who did not fit idealized standards in the United States and the United Kingdom along with an immediate feedback system asking for a response by text messaging. Next to the photos were two "tic-box" options that invited text votes on these women: Fit or Fat? Withered or Wonderful? Gray or Gorgeous? A rush of 1.5 million votes proved customer engagement,[12] and Dove has been helping women tell their stories of real beauty ever since.

---

12.   Nina Bahadur, "Dove 'Real Beauty' Campaign Turns 10: How a Brand Tried to Change the Conversation about Female Beauty," *Huffington Post*, March 14, 2014. Retrieved from http://www.huffingtonpost.com/2014/01/ 21/dove-real-beauty-campaign-turns-10_n_4575940.html.

There is never enough information or clarity to guarantee a story's success in the complexity of the real world, so we may as well throw it against the wall and see if it sticks. In product design, content marketing, and storytelling, if it works, it works. If you or your team are afraid to guess and test, you can't successfully adapt designs to human needs, write good content, or become good storytellers.

Experience-design manuals are full of exercises that facilitate story thinking and user focus. Here are two exercises I've adapted to use for generating innovative ideas for your next presentation.

> *Chance encounter*: Imagine a chance encounter with a friend or family member who loves and believes in you. Pretend this person is also a member of your audience who can make comments and ask questions during your talk. Run through your ideas or practice your talk in your mind as you simultaneously notice the reactions and questions your imagination prompts in your family/ friend. What did you learn?

> *Metaphor voyage*: Choose a metaphor to symbolize the outcome you desire for your audience. Do you want your audience to feel like they just woke up in a cool meadow? To burst into a fire of inspiration? To have a religious experience? Extend the metaphor by coming up with experiential elements. For instance, a cool-meadow morning might include experiences of lying on a blanket and watching a cricket in the warm sun. Next, let your imagination interpret these elements within the context of your future interaction.

For instance, you could validate existing beliefs using a nature-based metaphor that shines light on the topic and delivers the cool-meadow feeling. Or you might simulate a religious experience by adding an "altar call" feel to the end of your presentation by asking people to stand up and share a story they personally witnessed that gives them faith.

User experience (UX) design thinking has a lot to teach us about taking an "empathy field trip" to a user's (audience's) point of view. We need to relearn how to leave home and leave our assumptions and agendas in order to discover the things we don't know we don't know. Storytelling then becomes the ultimate disruptive technology.

Secrets from Singapore

Singapore's founders take their hard-won prosperity and racial/religious harmony very seriously. Born in conflict, this planned society was built for harmony. Government leaders sponsor storytellers to build Singaporean national values such as integrity, innovation, and social cohesion by telling approved stories in schools and communities.

Citizens can sign up to speak without preapproval about anything except race and religion at Speakers' Corner in Singapore. Elsewhere, storytellers are commissioned by the government or have a performer's license and preapproved story plots. While other performances are subject to script approval, storytellers only need plot approval so they can retain the spontaneity of cocreated stories.

Shortly before Singapore was formed in 1965, Alec Fraser-Brunner, curator of the Van Kleef Aquarium, designed a half-fish, half-lion symbol for the Singapore Tourist Promotion Board soon named the Merlion, now registered as a trademark. The government actively guides Merlion "myths" that artists can't help but invent. Rosemarie Somaiah, a professional storyteller who works in schools, told me that it is a kind, courageous Merlion who sometimes appears in her stories to save the day or point a character in the right direction. Apparently, myths do not need to be more than a thousand years old to work, and a good storyteller can invent new ones when needed.

Secrets from the Nonprofit World

At an economic level, giving to charity is defined as an irrational act driven by emotional reasoning. Every year, emotionally charged stories of compassion, guilt, love, and hate send hundreds of billions of US dollars to political and charitable nonprofits.[13] People donate because they experience themselves as heroes, helpers, or other characters in the stories nonprofits tell.

Good stories track core conflicts embedded in the human condition. Waterislife.com told stories that mined into conflicting themes with a series of videos that went viral. In each

---

13. National Philanthropic Trust, "Charitable Giving Statistics," January 16, 2015. Retrieved from http://www.nptrust.org/philanthropic-resources/charitable-giving-statistics.

scene, a disadvantaged person from a third-world country repeats excerpts from #firstworldproblems: A child stands in poverty and says, "I hate it when my phone-charger cord won't reach my bed." Another on the steps of a ruined building delivers the line, "I hate it when I go to write my maid a check, and I can't remember her last name." Consider weaving a story that juxtaposes core conflicts such as isolation versus belonging, innocence versus exploitation, or fairness versus deceit throughout your presentation.

What is at stake ultimately if you fail? When I teach storytelling to nutritionists, it is ultimately about life versus death as well as pleasure versus discomfort. For hairstylists, the stories run along the lines of isolation versus belonging and safety versus fear. At a military university recently, most stories I heard narrated the conflict between action and understanding. Once you discover what is at stake, you can craft your story to reflect a core conflict and stir high-stakes emotions. Choosing a core conflict provides a strong narrative that delivers consistency even as the stories change.

Secrets from the Legal Field

Bless their hearts, lawyers tell me that storytelling is beaten out of them in law school despite the common wisdom that "whoever tells the best story wins." So most lawyers learn about storytelling after law school. Books, workshops, and blogs about storytelling for lawyers offer many interesting insights. For instance, the first story a lawyer tells is "who I am and why I am here," and it begins in the parking lot.

Everything a trial lawyer does tells judge and jury who they are and why they are there: from parking lot etiquette (it might be a potential jury member who also wants that parking space) to tone of voice, facial expressions, clothing, and off-hand comments. Authenticity is vital, so smart lawyers share stories that either preinterpret a weakness in a strong way or preempt worst-case-scenario interpretations by marking the trail to a better interpretation. What stories do you tell your audience indirectly between the parking lot and the beginning of your presentation?

Visual storytelling is a big part of a lawyer's kit bag. The visual story told by side-by-side images of Apple and Samsung mobile phones was a major factor in Apple's lawsuit against Samsung accusing them of using Apple's iPhone design without permission. One slide with images of the two side by side created a powerful visual impression that they looked virtually the same. However, in an appeal, Samsung proved that Apple's lawyers had used a Samsung-owned image from Samsung's website without permission, and, worse, they had altered the image by cropping out the Samsung logo. This is a great example of how a tiny detail can make a huge difference. Such is the world of storytelling.

Lawyers have always used metaphors to guide understanding. The complexities of law are impossible to grasp without metaphors such as "parent corporation" or "fruit of the poisonous tree." I may be partial, but Southern lawyers seem to excel at finding metaphors that direct interpretation and stimulate retention as well as offer comic relief: "[T]he work of the Alabama legislature in the area of medical liability is a mule—the bastard offspring of intercourse among lawyers, legislators and lobbyists having no pride of ancestry and no hope of prosperity."[14]

In a more serious application, Professor Cathren Koehlert-Page[15] wrote a 2013 article in *Nebraska Law Review* titled "Like a Glass Slipper on a Step Sister: How the One Ring Rules Them All at Trial." She demonstrated how to anchor a metaphor by embedding it in an object to create a symbol. In one example, she describes how a wooden trap door admitted as evidence during the trial of mass murderer John Wayne Gacy turned into a meaningful symbol. This was the trap door Gacy installed over a freshly dug crawl space in which he disposed of his victim's bodies. The physical reality of the actual door not only demonstrated the time, effort, and premeditation that Gacy devoted to his murders, but the trap door also recalled the pathos of each victim's last moments as Gacy operated this door to let evil into the world.

What if you held a cell phone up to your nose every time you told a story about lost opportunities to connect face to face? This gesture could become a symbol to your audience in the future, so the next time they find themselves squinting at a cell phone, it triggers a desire to speak personally. J. J. Abrams used a "mystery box" he bought from a magicians store when he was a boy to symbolize the power of mystery in a 2007

14. Michael R. Smith, talking about Hayes v. Lucky 33 F. Supp. 2d. 987, 995, n16 (ND Ala. 1997); see Smith, "Levels of Metaphor in Persuasive Legal Writing," *Mercer Law Review*, 58(3), 2007. Retrieved from http://ssrn.com/abstract=1105901.

15. Cathren Koehlert-Page, "Like a Glass Slipper on a Stepsister: How the One Ring Rules Them All at Trial," *Nebraska Law Review*, 91, 2013. Retrieved from http://digitalcommons.unl.edu/nlr/vol91/iss3/3.

TED (Technology, Entertainment, Design) talk. What object or image might serve as a symbol of your message? When you combine the oratorical method of repetition with a visual or sensory stimulus, you can create a symbol embedded with meaning.

The Trial Lawyers College run by Gerry Spence, of Silkwood fame (in 1974, Karen Silkwood died in a mysterious car crash only six months after she testified before the Atomic Energy Commission about dangerous levels of plutonium at a Kerr-McGee fuel fabrication site), uses a process called "psychodrama" to teach lawyers about storytelling and subjective thinking. Lawyers learn to reenact critical events by directing and acting in a story told in the form of a reenactment or play. They can play the role of themselves or another character. The training begins when each lawyer portrays his or her own personal story and asks colleagues to play different roles. Each lawyer gets the chance to hear various versions of his or her own story as those who play a role share the experience and point of view witnessed from a different perspective.

Don't let the word *psychodrama* throw you off. It may sound a little too much like therapy, but it is really a high-value tool for story finding and story development. I've also seen professional storytellers such as Jay O'Callahan use a similar process to develop their stories. One time, when we were both participants in a storytelling workshop, Jay asked several of us to stand up and play characters in his story "Pouring the Sun," a tale about immigrant steelworkers. He benefited because those of us playing roles took places to stand as each character might stand, and it enabled him to see the scene more clearly in his mind's eye and improved his telling. I benefited because I got to stand in my character's strength, courage, and integrity to see the scene as she might have seen it. I can still feel her essence now.

Start by asking a few friends to help you block out one scene from a story you have told before, and ask them to notice something you might not have already noticed from your point of view. If it works well, you can segue a story into a role play simply by asking a few of your listeners to stand in as characters in your story. The stories you hear from your stand-in characters might reveal details that mean the difference between creating empathy and creating apathy.

Search for the keyword "psychodrama" to find courses and more information. I recommend calling it a reenactment in real life so people don't start whistling the theme to *The Twilight Zone*.

Secrets from Narrative Medicine

Doctors need to know a patient's story to make a diagnosis. Yet a massive shift to electronic health records often replaces patient stories with data points. Simultaneously, the average time doctors spend with patients continues to shrink. As a result, medical schools are getting better at teaching interview techniques so that doctors can find the hidden clues and emotional content embedded in patient stories.

When interviewing people to find stories, any of us can use the same techniques doctors use when interviewing patients. Don't interrupt the patient's opening statement. Look for verbal and nonverbal cues of charged emotion, zero in on those emotions, validate them with words of understanding, and glean the story behind them. Sometimes you have to bleed off charged emotions in order to hear a story. Don't ask questions that distract a patient's attention from his or her story because of your preconceived assumptions.

Psychiatrists and psychotherapists have long used "narrative therapy" to deepen self-awareness, shift perspectives, and find solutions within a patient's narrative of his or her disease, symptoms, and coping strategies. Therapist and patient collaboratively extract meaning from these narratives and test alternative meanings. New and improved narratives drive healthier behaviors and more sustainable thinking routines. Rita Charon, M.D. and Ph.D., founded the Program in Narrative Medicine at Columbia University Medical Center in order to legitimize and promote the value stories and narratives bring to medicine. Charon and her colleagues recommend that doctors keep a journal.

I heard an excerpt from one young doctor's journal on the radio more than a decade ago: "There was nothing left to do for her, but I stayed in her room anyway. I don't think anyone should die alone." When you keep a journal, you reflect daily on what is important enough to write down. For this woman, her important moment turned into an unforgettable story on the radio. If you don't keep a journal, you may forget details or never reflect on an event in a way that turns it into a powerful personal story.

At the edges of formal health care, patients and caregivers also trade stories on social media to crowdsource diagnoses, research treatments and diseases, find emotional support, and provide data to support research efforts. A mom who posted a picture of her sick child on Facebook along with a short story about her doctor's inconclusive diagnoses prompted a friend to recognize her own child's experience and suggest they test her for the same rare but deadly condition. The test was positive, and the Facebook comment probably saved the child's life. Facebook obviously wasn't designed to improve health care, but it and other social media platforms provide many opportunities to find, tell, share, and create stories.

Secrets from Digital Storytelling and Content Marketing

Big corporations now use stories to frame research, design software, and develop marketing and communication strategies. SAP hired a "chief storyteller." Microsoft now has a senior director of storytelling. The number of storytelling agencies and blogs has exploded. Excellent online courses and workshops offer immersive training in video, audio, photography, and editing software that propel you forward even if you have not yet discerned what story you wish to tell to whom or why. On the positive side, your unconscious mind is forced to take over, and you may be happily surprised at the end result. To me, digital storytelling includes all forms of electronic storytelling. The problem is that learning new software or chasing the latest cool technology can eat your time or suck you into a black hole of frustration that distracts you from developing your story using the original storytelling format: telling your story in person.

At a personal level, creating a digital story can be transformational in the same way that learning how to paint changes what you see. The experience helps you find your voice, delivers the catharsis of telling an untold story, and forces you to review assumptions it may be time to change. Not all personal digital stories deliver a transformational experience to others, but the benefits of creating a digital story can be their own reward.

I highly recommend you begin with a for-your-eyes-only digital story with as many special effects, transitions, audio effects, and images as you can shove into two minutes, just to get your feet wet and experience the process. For me, it was like holding my nose and jumping in the deep end. I both hated it and loved it. Learning the technology launched an explosion of creative ideas and better insight into my story and storytelling process.

Joe Lambert of the Center for Digital Storytelling (CDS) has been teaching digital storytelling for more than 20 years. His CDS workshops range from three to five days and facilitate several opportunities for participants to tell oral versions of their stories as they work through internal emotions and group responses to find the essence of their stories before introducing any aspects of script, storyboard, or technical considerations. Individual and group reflection are just as important to designing a successful digital story as understanding the technology. For more details, you can download a CDS *Digital Storytelling Cookbook* at storycenter.org or sign up for a workshop. Joe's focus on civil rights means that the process is well suited for developing your authentic voice and truth telling.

Likewise, if members of a group have not yet found their voice or agreed on who they are, why they exist, and faced the differences between professed stories and lived stories, creating a digital story can be transformative as well—but not necessarily in the right direction. If you don't first facilitate your group in a dialogue that creates or confirms a congruent who/why story before jumping into digital media, you can waste a lot of time. When a CEO, CFO, product manager, and sales manager hold different internal versions of what a company's story should be, conflicts over the infinite options of digital tools, tactics, and tone mask the core problem and compromise the end result.

Workshops with traditional oral storytellers rarely lose sight of the transformational process of codiscovering wisdom and cocreating collaborative experiences. Digital storytelling adds layers of decisions about sound, images, and edits, often with a steep learning curve. The process is the same, however. Find your story. Decide how to tell it. Test it several times. Refine it based on feedback about what works.

If the story is good to begin with, the expanded toolkit of digital storytelling can paint it vividly and deliver it where oral storytelling can't go. However, it's hard to punch up a weak story no matter how many bells and whistles you use.

One last thing to consider is that many digital storytellers claim that digital storytelling enables you to use "nontraditional" forms that are more interactive than other media. I think this overlooks the fact that nothing could be more traditional than interactive storytelling.

Digital storytelling may shift the timing from simultaneous interaction to asynchronous interaction, but interaction has always been a fundamental part of oral storytelling. Traditional storytellers call it audience participation, as they invite the audience to add sound effects, sing, decide what happens next, play a character in the story, or even play a game within the context of a story. You will find an infinite variety of creative ideas when you realize you can make all these old traditions new again.

Secrets from Storytelling Podcasts like *This American Life*, *The Moth*, and *Serial*

The most important secret about storytelling podcasts is that listening to them will improve your storytelling by osmosis. Because stories are cocreated in your mind as you listen, your brain is learning what tactics best manufacture images and sensations in your mind's eye. *Serial*, the podcast that rocketed to number one in 2014, told one true story in 12 weekly episodes and proved once and for all that people will make time to listen to long stories if they are told well. There are also excellent videos of storytellers from *The Moth*, TED, and other sources. Watch or listen to your favorite stories more than once and list specific techniques/ideas you would like to try. Trust your intuition to find ideas that will work best for your style of storytelling. Beware of advice meant to work for everyone.

Many successful storytelling podcast websites offer storytelling advice that represents their particular journey to success in their particular medium. That doesn't mean the advice isn't helpful; it just means that different approaches work for different people in different media and that genius storytellers don't always understand their own genius. One notable exception is the unanimous good advice to regain momentum by delivering a surprise.

For a performance-level story or film, these experts recommend we discover what is at stake and make sure the stakes are high. A victim story rarely creates a compelling story unless that victim overcomes some obstacle—the hero story. Still, there is a place in the story when you want to hook your listener's limbic system into panicking a bit when things are going terribly wrong or something of great importance might be lost. Many business stories are too tidy. The traditional case study, with its implicit ending that everything turned out OK, is boring. Only by bringing in personalities and frustration can you find a way to surprise your listener or reader. It is when none of the alternatives are good that you can create enough suspense that your audience leans in to wonder what details matter and engage in "what would I do?" speculation.

High stakes might include a relationship, personal integrity, a father's love, self-respect, justice, faith, or hope. Even a simple anecdote is embedded with a conflict of values if you look hard enough. *South Park* creators Trey Parker and Matt Stone suggest that every scene transition with either "therefore" or "but" as a way to ensure that every scene is transactional in building details and events that support what is at stake (therefore) or what is threatening (but). Refining a story to traverse high stakes and loss often helps craft a story with emotional impact.

Storytelling podcasts bring you exceptionally good stories, but remember that they reject far more stories than they tell. Ira Glass of *This American Life* says that the team spends half its time rejecting story ideas. *Moth* storytellers are hand selected from hundreds of people with story pitches and have often been coached for more than a year before they tell their stories on the main stage. So be gentle with yourself. Enjoy and absorb all the "new" storytellers, stories, and storytelling advice, but remember to trust your personal experiences of telling and listening to stories to stay close to what is meaningful to you, your peers, and your target audience. You are ultimately the only expert on the best way to tell your personal stories.

Teaching Storytelling

THE BEST MEASURE of success for a storytelling workshop is not some encyclopedic grasp of story theory but a significant increase in the number and quality of stories found and told posttraining. For this reason, it doesn't make sense to teach storytelling without first addressing self-censorship. High performers who aren't keen to embrace vulnerability and risk anxieties can tend to narrow their story experiments to safe bets and safety nets and forfeit the opportunity to experience the emotional impact of telling edgier stories with more contrast and self-disclosure.

I recommend you address these barriers up front, beginning with your own Who-I-Am and Why-I-Am-Here stories. The second trick I use is to dive into simple storytelling and listening experiences that demonstrate in real time that participants already know how to tell emotionally relevant stories. Reducing these barriers while you build a sense of competence increases everyone's chances to build skills and explore a variety of applications for storytelling.

As you tell your own stories, explain that every human being is a good storyteller in the sense that every belief, opinion, and memory is a story. Be transparent. Don't overpromise the value of templates or guidelines. They are as useful as a diet book is to a person who is overweight: technically accurate but insufficient to produce results. Knowing what you should do is useless unless you feel like doing it and develop a feel for doing it. Templates and guidelines are not as valuable as developing the skill to see how emotional reasoning works in yourself and others.

You teach far more than storytelling in this way. The same principles that improve storytelling also develop leadership, emotional intelligence, self-examination, and communication skills across the board. When you teach storytelling with this process, you are also teaching participants a new way to think. Participants learn to understand others by mapping the mental terrain of those they seek to influence. They learn how to develop a communication strategy that addresses both facts and feelings. They acquire visceral memories of the power of authenticity that will translate into habits of authenticity.

The following timeline is not meant to suggest you start at 9 a.m. sharp; it is simply a way to communicate sequence and emphasis.

Prepare for the Introductions Process

I have collected more than 150 postcards with images that represent common human dilemmas. I recommend you start your own collection. I lay the postcards on the floor and ask participants, "Please choose a postcard with an image that explains your role/daily work environment."

This gets people thinking in images: a great way to open up the imagination and leave distractions behind. You could also offer six or seven funny animal pictures on a PowerPoint slide. Any images will do, as long as they portray emotions likely to be experienced at work (happy, sad, frustrated, connected, confused, or stressed).

9:00 a.m.: Credibility and Rapport

Begin with a couple of Who-I-Am and Why-I-Am-Here stories. You need to have several who/why stories ready to go before you even think about teaching storytelling. For that matter, you need one each from the six kinds of stories and one each from the buckets: shined, blew it, mentor, and book/movie/event. The process of finding, developing, and polishing a dozen of your own stories will earn you credibility and dramatically improve your ability to facilitate this process.

9:15 a.m.: Practice for the Imagination/Introductions

Let participants introduce themselves by sharing the image they chose with a short explanation: "My role is. . . . It is like . . . because. . . ."

If you have a large group, people can share with a partner for two minutes each, and you can ask partners to nominate the "really good ones" to share with the larger group. I don't offer a definition of "really good" but encourage people to trust their instincts and discuss where their instincts led them afterward.

9:30 a.m.: Story Definition and Five Senses

Define *story* as a narrated experience that feels real to both the teller and listener. Sometimes I narrate a vivid description of biting into a lemon and then ask who had a physiological reaction.

The point here is to keep everyone attuned to how our physical bodies interpret reality. No matter what the frontal lobes think, the body mostly trusts what it sees, hears, smells, tastes, and touches. Tell a few stories with vibrant sensory details about an accomplished business goal and then ask the group to recall images, sounds, smells, tastes, and visceral sensations.

People may want to hear a bit of the science behind storytelling to comfort their need for objective proof. A quick search will turn up information on mirror neurons, neuron coupling, and more. You can tell the farmer story from Chapter 1 to demonstrate that beginnings and endings are arbitrary and "truth" is subject to the story as we see and believe it.

9:45 a.m.: Objective/Subjective Model

Critical thinking trained us to think in ways that minimize emotions and imagination. I usually ask, "Have you ever been right and still no one listened to you?" or "Have you ever gotten in trouble for telling the truth?"

This is because coming up with the right answer does not mean people will listen to you. Zero in on this universal human experience to spur curiosity and increase tolerance for the idea that critical thinking is not always the best way to think.

Project the vase/faces illusion (Chapter 1) and ask the group to comment. Ask them to try to see both at the same time. It is neurologically impossible. Describe how seeing the people can make the object "disappear" for a second. It's still there when you come back to it. This image not only illustrates that the perspective for seeing facts is different from the perspective for seeing feelings, but it also anticipates the discomfort of temporarily suspending critical thinking routines.

Promise the participants that they can always revert back to critical thinking, but storytelling is a function of subjective thinking. Finding stories and crafting stories are best done from the perspective of seeing people rather than critical analysis.

I rarely present all the elements in the following model, but I tell a story for every element I present. You will see an asterisk beside the ones I consider vital.

Objective Reality	Subjective Reality
Facts*	Feelings*
Right or wrong (via measurements)	Connection, collaboration, influence
True or false—scientific method*	Experience—it depends*
Linear—99.6 Percent guaranteed*	Nonlinear—guess and test*
Recipe	Box of kittens
Rules (that tell you the difference)	Wisdom (to know the difference)
Consistency (standardized policy)	Kindness (making exceptions)
It doesn't matter how people feel.*	The most important thing is how people feel.*

When you make a distinction between facts and feelings, make sure you validate the role that objective thinking and critical thinking play in our everyday lives. No one is saying critical or objective thinking is not important. We are simply saying that subjective thinking skills have been ignored and may have deteriorated, so it is necessary to reinvest time stimulating story-thinking skills, particularly the role of intuition. Reiterate that in order to find good stories and tell them with vibrancy, we have to temporarily disable critical thinking habits that kill baby stories so we can tap into intuition, empathy, and wisdom.

One way to explain the first point about facts and feelings, as well as deliver a burst of self-confidence, is to ask participants to tell a pet story: "OK . . . we are going to tell a story about a pet. It doesn't have to be your pet; any pet story will do. Find a partner. You each have two minutes. Go!"

The best way to get people to share stories with the whole group is to let them share with a partner first and then ask partners to nominate stories they think the group should hear. This way you provide a low-risk story practice opportunity; plus, the stories that are nominated include people who might have great stories but are too shy to share. Inevitably, the nominated stories are wonderful, and it teaches everyone that "charisma" isn't the secret to storytelling.

After the pet stories, ask the group, "Do you feel different? What changed?"

People usually describe the experience as an increase in energy and feelings of connection. It doesn't matter what a story is about; if it changes the emotions of the group, it changes what happens next.

Ask for nominations and get a couple of people to share their stories.

Once the group notices the shift in emotion and energy, point out that feelings alter perceptions of facts. Give some examples, and ask for examples from the group.

Point out the following: "If you walk into a room full of unhappy people who think no one cares about their opinions and present your facts and figures, how do they view these facts? Cynicism and suspicion can cause people to discredit your facts. They may attack your research methodology or question the source. On the other hand, enthusiasm can cause people to supersize your facts. Feelings are more powerful than facts. Facts may help people think, but emotion ('to move out' from the original Latin) controls behavior and how people define what is and is not a fact."

In order to distract people from wanting a clear recipe for storytelling, I give this example:

> If I wanted to get people's attention, I'd bring in a box of kittens. There is statistical evidence that people like kittens. Pretend we've got a box of kittens in the middle of the room. One is chasing his sister. Another has jumped out and is playing with someone's shoelaces. Where would most people's attention be directed? (Nothing is 100 percent; some people don't like cats.)
>
> Voila. I have found the secret to getting attention. But what if I want to "scale" this phenomenon and replicate it in other situations? The scientific method leads me to believe that if I analyze it, I will understand it.

So I should cut a kitten in half and examine its com-
ponents, right? But what have I done? I have destroyed
that which I seek to understand. Forcing an analysis on
storytelling—the language of emotions—destroys that
which you seek to understand.

At this point, people get grossed out. Vivid sensory images
like this make your ideas more vivid. Be silly and have fun with
it, but long pauses work better than lots of detail on this one.
You don't want to incite a gagging response.

Using the previous two examples, you can figure out the
rest by yourself. Spend up to 30 minutes building the group's
"perceptual agility" so they can escape the barriers to storytelling for the rest of the session.

By this time, you may have a few critical thinkers who are
feeling restless (even fewer if you've been telling great stories).
They may criticize this process as lacking focus and structure.
You can explain that stories are about context (the opposite
of focus) and experience (destroyed when summarized into
recipes). But they've been patient, and it is time to deliver a
storytelling lesson and practice.

10:15 a.m.: Story Practice: Choose the Core Message

Explain the six kinds of stories and then zero in on finding
a Who-I-Am/Why-I-Am-Here story. It's a twofer because
stories often reveal something about who you are as well as
why you are here. In workshops, I combine the two. You
want participants to remember that listeners who have
decided you are a good person and who believe you are there
for the right reasons are much easier to influence. Therefore,

who/why stories are useful in any situation where they seek to influence others.

At some point, I explain that we practice three-minute stories. The business environment values brevity. If we assume that up to 30 percent of their stories will miss the mark, then the discipline of three-minute stories ensures that if it's not working, it will be over soon!

Ask participants to write down three qualities that earn them the right to influence their particular target audience. Remind them not to pick a situation that seems hopeless for their first practice story.

Once they have written the three qualities and start looking for a story, suggest they stop worrying about audience and simply find the best story that reveals their internal qualities. Alert them to how their inner critical voice may be overly cautious and prematurely discard perfectly good stories as irrelevant or inappropriate.

10:30 a.m.: Story Finding: Four Buckets

Introduce the four buckets for finding stories by telling your own stories of a time you shined, a time you blew it, a mentor, and a book/movie/current event (as described in Chapter 3). When you give a story, you get a story. So your success depends on how well your stories stimulate their stories. When you model spontaneity, authenticity, recovering from a flub, and comfort with ambiguity and experiments, you not only teach these principles but expand them. Ask the group to jot down any story ideas that occur to them.

10:45 a.m.: Writing the Bones of the Story

Ask the participants to spend a silent five minutes writing down the bones of one story idea. Ask them to reexperience the event in their imagination and take as many notes as they can on images, sounds, tastes, smells, and sensations. They may only use a fraction of the details they record, but the more details they record, the better their stories will be.

10:50 a.m.: Share Your Story with a Partner

Explain that baby stories need a first run with a friendly listener. Ask each participant to test a baby story and to listen to himself or herself tell it to a friendly listener. Instruct listeners that saying things such as "OMG, I used to live in Denver too!" is not listening. Ask them to listen with delight, in silence. Listening with delight expands the creative space as tellers improvise and play around with dialogue, details, and timing.

Explain that some will finish before three minutes, and some will still be talking at the three-minute mark.

> For listeners of those who finish early, keep listening so your partner can try to fill in the silence. Sometimes filling in this silence makes a good story a great story. Those who run out of time, you know what your lesson is. Brevity is a gift.

11:00 a.m.: Experiencing Story Success and Skills via Teachable Moments

The beauty of teaching storytelling is watching people discover that they already have good stories and know how to tell them. So make sure they notice!

Ask, "Who just heard a good story?" Most participants will raise their hands. Ask them to look around and notice how many good stories and good storytellers were already in the room. Take advantage of the raised hands and ask people to consider nominating a particularly good story for the entire room to hear. The next step seems soft to people used to critical feedback, but it takes more courage to stick with identifying what works than to slip into suggestions or critique.

> See? You already know how to do this. You have a natural ability to recognize a story that packs an emotional punch. Who will nominate a really good story so we can do the next step in the process for developing a story? There are great stories out there. Please point out the ones who told those great stories. We want to learn what worked so we can remember to do it again.

Make sure you have a format for appreciations up on a screen or on handouts.

"What your story tells me about you is. . . ."

"The sensory details I like in your story are. . . ."

"What your story helps me remember is. . . ."

"The impact I can see your story having in (describe specific situation) is. . . ."

Reiterate that tellers don't need to hear what didn't work, and they particularly don't need to hear what "someone else" might misunderstand. Ask participants to share only their personal experience of a teller's story and to stick to the format of appreciations. Use the content in Part 3 of this book to elaborate on particular storytelling skills and strategies done well in participant stories.

Spend the rest of the session sharing stories and appreciations. Ideally, this will be the last hour of the session, but depending on your group size, situation, and background, it could be the last 15 minutes. Trust your intuition, and never lose faith that all participants will have positive storytelling experiences if you can show them how to get out of their own way and help them see what they are already doing well.

Bibliography

Angelou, Maya. *I Know Why the Caged Bird Sings*. New York: Bantam, 1973.
————. *Singin' and Swingin' and Gettin' Merry Like Christmas*. New York: Bantam, 1997.
————. *A Song Flung up to Heaven*. New York: Bantam, 2003.
Armstrong, Karen. *A Short History of Myth*. New York: Canongate, 2005.
Bahadur, Nina. "Dove 'Real Beauty' Campaign Turns 10: How a Brand Tried to Change the Conversation about Female Beauty," *Huffington Post*, March 14, 2014. Retrieved from http://www.huffingtonpost.com/2014/01/21/dove-real-beauty-campaign-turns-10_n_4575940.html.
Brodie, Richard. *Virus of the Mind: The New Science of the Meme*. Seattle, Wash.: Integral Press, 1996.
Bruner, Jerome. *Acts of Meaning*. Cambridge, MA: Harvard University Press, 1990.
Buckley, Cara. "Ira Glass's 'This American Life' Leaves PRI," *The New York Times*, July 2, 2014. Retrieved from http://www.nytimes.com/2014/07/06/arts/ira-glasss-this-american-life-leaves-pri.html.
Cash, Johnny. *Cash: The Autobiography*. New York: HarperOne, 2003.
Cialdini, Robert. *Influence: Science and Practice*. Boston: Allyn and Bacon, 2001.
Cleveland, Harlan. *Nobody in Charge: Essays on the Future of Leadership*. San Francisco: Jossey-Bass, 2002.
Close, Henry T. *Metaphor in Psychotherapy: Clinical Applications of Stories and Allegories*. San Luis Obispo, Calif.: Impact, 1998.
Collins, Jim. *Good to Great: Why Some Companies Make the Leap . . . and Others Don't*. New York: HarperCollins, 2001.
Cooper, Alan, Robert Reimann, and Dave Cronin. *About Face 3: The Essentials of Interaction Design*. Indianapolis, Ind.: Wiley, 2007.
Cooper, Robert K., and Ayman Sawaf. *Executive EQ: Emotional Intelligence in Leadership and Organizations*. New York: Grosset/Putnam, 1997.

Cron, Lisa. *Wired for Story: The Writer's Guide to Using Brain Science to Hook Readers from the Very First Sentence*. Berkeley: Ten Speed, 2012.

Davies, Andrew. "Coca-Cola Marketing: The Future," *idio blog*, February 9, 2013. Retrieved from http://www.idioplatform.com/coca-cola-content-marketing-is -the-future-2.

De Ciantis, Cheryl, and Kenton Hyatt. *What's Important: Understanding and Working with Values Perspectives*. Tucson, Ariz.: Integral Publishers, 2014.

Downs, Alan. *The Half-Empty Heart: A Supportive Guide to Breaking Free from Chronic Discontent*. New York: St. Martins, 2004.

———. *Secrets of an Executive Coach: Proven Methods for Helping Leaders Excel under Pressure*. New York: AMACOM, 2002.

Duarte, Nancy. *Persuasive Presentations*. Boston: Harvard Business Review, 2012.

———. *Resonate: Present Visual Stories that Transform Audiences*. Hoboken, N.J.: John Wiley and Sons, 2010.

Fähling, Jens, Michael Huber, Felix Böhm, Jan Marco Leimeister, and Helmut Krcmar. "Scenario Planning for Innovation Development: An Overview of Different Innovation Domains," *International Journal of Technology Intelligence and Planning (IJTIP)*, 8(2), 2012: 95–114.

Feudtner, Chris. "Patients' Stories and Clinical Care: Uniting the Unique and the Universal?" *Journal of General Internal Medicine*, 13(12), December 1998: 846–49. Retrieved from http://www.ncbi.nlm.nih.gov/pmc/articles/PMC1497037.

Forman, Janice. *Storytelling in Business*. Stanford, Calif.: Stanford University Press, 2013.

Gilbert, Daniel. *Stumbling on Happiness*. New York: Alfred Knopf, 2006.

Gladwell, Malcolm. *Blink: The Power of Thinking without Thinking*. Boston: Little, Brown, 2005.

———. *The Tipping Point: How Little Things Can Make a Big Difference*. Boston: Little, Brown, 2000.

Glimcher, Paul W. *Decisions, Uncertainty, and the Brain: The Science of Neuroeconomics*. Cambridge, Mass.: MIT Press, 2004.

Godin, Seth. *All Marketers Are Liars: The Power of Telling Authentic Stories in a Low-Trust World*. London: Penguin, 2005.

———. *Permission Marketing: Turning Strangers into Friends and Friends into Customers*. New York: Simon and Schuster, 1999.

Goleman, Daniel. *Emotional Intelligence: Why It Can Matter More than IQ*. New York: Bantam, 1995.

Gottschall, Jonathan. *The Storytelling Animal: How Stories Make Us Human*. New York: Houghton Mifflin Harcourt, 2011.

Harrell, Cyd, and Jodi Leo. "Metaphorical Analysis: The Powerful Research Technique You're Not Using," *UX Magazine*, April 19, 2013. Retrieved from https://uxmag.com/articles/metaphorical-analysis.

Heath, Chip, and Dan Heath. *Switch: When Change Is Hard*. New York: Random House, 2010.

Hinton, Andrew. "The Story Is the Thing," *UX Storytellers: Connecting the Dots*. Ed. Jan Jursa. Retrieved from http://www.scribd.com/doc/40698393/UX-Storytellers.

Katherine, Anne. *Where to Draw the Line: How to Set Health Boundaries Every Day*. New York: Fireside, 2000.

Koehlert-Page, Cathren. "Like a Glass Slipper on a Stepsister: How the One Ring Rules Them All at Trial," *Nebraska Law Review*, 91, 2013. Retrieved from http://digitalcommons.unl.edu/nlr/vol91/iss3/3.

Lakoff, George. *Don't Think of an Elephant! Know Your Values and Frame the Debate: The Essential Guide for Progressives*. White River Junction, Vt.: Chelsea Green, 2004.

Lamott, Annie. *Bird by Bird: Some Instructions on Writing and Life*. New York: Anchor, 1994.

Langer, Ellen J. *Mindfulness*. Reading, MA: Addison-Wesley, 1989.

———. *On Becoming an Artist: Reinventing Yourself through Mindful Creativity*. New York: Ballantine, 2005.

———. *The Power of Mindful Learning*. Reading, Mass.: Addison-Wesley, 1997.

Lawrence-Lightfoot, Sara. *Respect: An Exploration*. Reading, Mass.: Perseus, 2000.

LeDoux, Joseph. *The Emotional Brain: The Mysterious Underpinning of Emotional Life*. New York: Touchstone, 1996.

Levitt, Steven, and Stephen Dubner. *Freakonomics: A Rogue Economist Explores the Hidden Side of Everything*. New York: HarperCollins, 2005.

Lewis, C. S. *Surprised by Joy: The Shape of My Early Life*. London: Fontana, 1956.

Lipman, Doug. *Improving Your Storytelling: Beyond the Basics for All Who Tell Stories in Work or Play*. Little Rock, Ark.: August House, 1999.

———. *The Storytelling Coach*. Atlanta: August House, 1995.

Lohr, Steve. "Unblinking Eyes Track Employees, Seeing Both Good and Bad," *The New York Times*, June 22, 2014. Retrieved from http://www.nytimes.com/2014/07/06/arts/ira-glasss-this-american-life-leaves-pri.html?_r=1.

Mayhew, Deborah J. "Ux Then and Now," *UX Storytellers: Connecting the Dots*. Ed. Jan Jursa. Retrieved from http://www.scribd.com/doc/40698393/UX-Storytellers.

Meyer, Phillip N. *Storytelling for Lawyers*. New York: Oxford University Press, 2014.

Mezzick, Daniel. *The Culture Game: Tools for the Agile Manager*. Lexington, Ky.: Freestanding, 2012.

Mighall, Robert. *Only Connect: The Art of Corporate Storytelling*. London: LID, 2013.

National Philanthropic Trust. "Charitable Giving Statistics," January 16, 2015. Retrieved from http://www.nptrust.org/philanthropic-resources/charitable-giving-statistics.

Ornstein, Robert. *The Right Mind: Making Sense of the Hemispheres*. San Diego: Harvest, 1997.

Pert, Candace B. *Molecules of Emotion: Why You Feel the Way You Feel*. New York: Scribner, 1997.

Robbins, Ruth Anne. *Your Client's Story: Persuasive Legal Writing*. Waltham, Mass.: Aspen, 2012.

Rose, Billy. "The Unknown Soldier," *The Best Loved Poems of the American People*. Ed. Hazel Felleman. Garden City, NY: Doubleday, 1936.

Schank, Roger C. *Tell Me a Story: Narrative and Intelligence*. Evanston, Ill.: Northwestern University Press, 1998.

Schank, Roger, and Ellen Langer, eds. *Beliefs, Reasoning, and Decision Making*. Mahwah, N.J.: Lawrence Erlbaum, 1994.

Seligman, Martin. *What You Can Change and What You Can't: Learning to Accept Who You Are*. New York: Fawcett Columbine, 1993.

Senge, Peter, C. Otto Scharmer, Joseph Jaworski, and Betty Sue Flowers. *Presence: An Exploration of Profound Change in People, Organizations, and Society*. New York: Doubleday, 2005.

Shan-Loong, Mark Lim. "'Shared Values' and Their Role in Singapore's Evolving Ideological Framework," March 26, 1999. Retrieved from http://marklsl.tripod.com/Writings/values.htm.

Signorelli, Jim. *Storybranding 2.0: Creating Standout Brands through the Power of Story*. Austin, Tex.: Greenleaf, 2012.

Simmons, Annette. *A Safe Place for Dangerous Truths: Using Dialogue to Overcome Fear and Distrust at Work*. New York: AMACOM, 1999.

———. *The Story Factor: Inspiration, Influence and Persuasion through the Art of Storytelling*, 2nd ed. Boston: Basic, 2006.

———. *Territorial Games: Understanding and Ending Turf Wars*. New York: AMACOM, 1998.

Smith, Michael R. "Levels of Metaphor in Persuasive Legal Writing," *Mercer Law Review*, 58(3), 2007. Retrieved from http://ssrn.com/abstract=1105901.

Suroweicki, James. *The Wisdom of Crowds*. New York: Doubleday, 2004.

Tan, Eugene. "Singapore Shared Values," *Singapore Infopedia*, 2015. Retrieved from National Library of Singapore website, http://eresources.nlb.gov.sg/infopedia/articles/SIP_542_2004-12-18.html.

Taylor, William C. "Get Out of That Rut and into the Shower," *The New York Times*, August 13, 2006.

Walsh, Stephen H. "The Clinician's Perspective on Electronic Health Records and How They Can Affect Patient Care," *BMJ : British Medical Journal*, 328(7449), 2004: 1184–87. Retrieved from http://www.ncbi.nlm.nih.gov/pubmed/15142929.

Watts, Nigel. *Writing a Novel*. London: Hodder Education, 2006.

Wilson, Chauncey. "Method 5 of 100: Metaphor Brainstorming, 100 User Experience (UX) Design and Evaluation Methods for Your Toolkit," *Autodesk Blog*, February 1, 2011. Retrieved from http://dux.typepad.com/dux/2011/02/this-is-the-5th-in-a-series-of-100-short-articles-about-ux-design-and-evaluation-methods-todays-method-is-called-metaphor.html.

Zipes, Jack. "Chapter One: The Cultural Evolution of Storytelling and Fairy Tales," *The Irresistible Fairy Tale: The Cultural and Social History of a Genre*. Princeton, N.J.: Princeton University Press, 2010. Retrieved from http://press.princeton.edu/titles/9676.html..

Index

About the Author

Annette Simmons believes in helping businesses, marketers, and institutions of every stripe uncover their truths and tell them. She has pursued this goal for two decades, working with leadership teams across the world as diverse as the Pentagon, the Brookings Institute, Microsoft, Best Buy, and PricewaterhouseCoopers.

Her first two books focused on uncovering truth within organizations. *A Safe Place for Dangerous Truth* (1998) and *Territorial Games: Understanding and Ending Turf Wars at Work* (1997) showed how to reveal hidden agendas and unproductive internal "stories" and how to better manage group dynamics so teams can thrive and flourish.

This experience taught her the emotional impact of telling your story—the clarity and power a story brings to messages of every kind. Her groundbreaking book *The Story Factor* (2001) was named by 1-800-CEO-Read as one of *The 100 Best Business Books of All Time* (Penguin, 2009), and her books have been translated into 11 languages. Today, she continues to deliver keynotes, consultations, and training to help individuals and organizations tell true stories that win both hearts and minds. Annette lives back in her hometown of Shreveport, Louisiana, with Lucy, an Italian Greyhound of substance and style.

Connect with Annette Simmons:
    Phone: (318) 861-9220
    E-Mail: Annette@annettesimmons.com
    Twitter: @TheStoryFactor